[1]

CONTENTS

FOREWARD

There have been many books written about Elvis, a lot have been sensationalised lies and half-truths, some are total fantasy, there have been a few good ones, but nowhere near as many as the bad ones. Some written by people he knew, some written by people who were not even born when he was alive and some making extraordinary unbelievable claims from people who have no knowledge of what they are peddling, all they care about is making money. The greed surrounding this kind, gentle, man since his death is quite horrific.

One book, by a woman who has no medical knowledge or proof, who refused to have any of Elvis's cousins tested, because she knew it would blow her A1alpha theory out of the water, said Elvis was destined to die, because he was an inbred country hick, the same as his mother, a title Elvis hated and struggled against his whole life. Another proclaimed with his book 'things only a brother would know', but he was not Elvis's brother, in fact he never spoke to or saw Elvis after 1972 (when Elvis changed the most) after he accused Elvis of sleeping with his wife, which Elvis did not. Elvis deserved none of this, he was a gentle, kind, caring man who would help anyone, as he said all he wanted to do was make people happy.

I want to try and dispel some of the myths and lies and show who Elvis really was on the inside, the side of him he shared with only a few, none of the macho crap talked about by some and not the image portrayed by his management but the real Elvis, the one he mostly had to hide for fear of ridicule or fear of upsetting those who could not understand. I am quite aware many will call me mad, and to quote Elvis: - "People think you are crazy when you talk about things they don't understand", some will call me a liar or fantasist or both, but this is my opinion. I can assure you I would never say anything that would hurt Elvis unlike so many others. I know he is watching from spirit and listening to everything said about him, I can only feel sorry for those who are eroding their souls with all those lies just for gain be it monetary or fame.

I hope I can show you who Elvis really was underneath and why he was how he was so that people will then understand him more and the gentle, kind, soul he really was. I know there are somethings I have repeated under different headings, it is because I think it is important.

This is Elvis as I knew him to be, how I saw him, as I stated, this is my opinion from what I have observed, seen, and read. Nearly everything in this book can either be found on the internet in other books, magazine, and newspaper articles and occasionally things that have been told to me personally by those who knew Elvis. I have put them all together to form this book, to shed light on who Elvis really was and who I think Elvis was in my words.

CHAPTER ONE

Elvis's quote,

"THE IMAGE IS ONE THING AND THE HUMAN BEING IS ANOTHER. IT'S VERY HARD TO LIVE UP TO AN IMAGE, PUT IT THAT WAY."

EVERYONE KNOWS ELVIS

The name Elvis Presley is known throughout the world as being the king of rock and roll, a singer, but he was much more than just a singer as all his humanitarian awards show and now over 45 years after his death his influence is felt around the globe not only by his millions of fans but by every person who has ever listened to popular music or gone to a protest or used their right to stand up and be counted.

A dirt poor boy, born on the wrong side of the tracks, bullied at school for being different, told he had no potential by his teachers, even told he could not sing, thrown out of the football team because he was different and would not conform to their idea of normal, against all the odds he stood firm to whom he was and would not change to suit the small minds and bigotry around him at that time.

When he embarked by chance on his singing career white stations would not play his records because he sounded black, black stations would not play him because he was white, piles of his records were burnt in the streets, even effigies of him were burnt, and he was called the devil incarnate and evil, a subversive, but he would not conform, he stayed true to himself, he did not just open doors between blacks and whites with his music he smashed down walls and tore up the foundations of the music industry itself,

Elvis was the catalyst for change, every popular black singer from that day on owed their success in a world that had been barred to them to Elvis, as many have testified on video and every black and white singer since, for Elvis laid down a new foundation for not only popular music but society as a whole, he gave the young generation of the time a voice, a voice of their own they had not had before, as one quote went, "every man wanted to be him and every woman wanted him", he influenced a whole generation to change and that change carried on, they had a voice, a voice they did not have before and all because this poor bullied boy had courage, more courage than most can imagine and a voice he would not change to suit the small-minded doctrine of the time, he is a shining example of what one person can do and how they can change society forever, could you imagine the teens of the early 50s before Elvis having the courage to take to the streets and demonstrate against things like war and poverty, no, they would not have dared, but Elvis set them free. He even influenced people in places that were not supposed to have freedom, like places behind the iron curtain they huddled round their radios to listen to him and even learned English so they could know what he was singing about, he set them free from the doctrine in their countries and gave them hope, hope, such a priceless gift.

Elvis was also a man who never forgot his humble beginnings and gave countless millions to charities of all kinds, some known, some anonymously, he also did concerts for charity, even the scarves he gave away every one of them made money for charity, and he paid for people in need to have operations they could not afford, not for publicity or fame but because he knew what it was like to have nothing and wanted to share his fortune with others, he would even give gifts of cars and motorbikes to complete strangers just to bring them joy, he never thought himself better than anyone else and always treated all people with respect and humility, for his fans he is more than a singer he is someone they respect and look up to, someone to emulate, he has unified countless millions across the world no matter where they come from, what nationality, religion, colour or creed they are unified because of one man, Elvis Presley, and in this 46th year since his death still the legions of his supporters grow, who else has ever had such a strong following. His story is the epitome of what one dirt-poor bullied boy who would not conform can do and is an inspiration to millions. Elvis Presley showed all those other poor bullied children what one American can do and give them hope and the courage to be great too, after all hope and courage are the greatest gifts anyone can give. On an English B.B.C. TV program 'Great American Railroad Journeys'

Michael Portillo said Elvis was one of the three greatest Americans to ever have lived.

Personally, I think Elvis was one of the greatest men who ever lived, he changed the whole world. A quote from Muhammad Ali. He said, "I was in Africa, and I went into this tent and there was nobody there, nothing but a holy bible. I picked it up and inside was a photo of Elvis!"

ELVIS THE MAN, HIS REAL CHARACTER. AND NOT THE IMAGE

The image most people have of Elvis is wrong sadly, many still think he was his image, but he was not.

This is what my Elvis was and as with so many other things you may or may not agree with me, but this is my opinion on him, my take on the real Elvis this is about him.

Elvis Presley said, "The image is one thing, and the human being is another. It's very hard to live up to an image, put it that way."

ELVIS WOULD RATHER READ TO SOMEONE FROM A SPIRITUAL BOOK OR SING TO THEM, OR JUST TALK.

Sadly, some people still believe the hype that Elvis was over-sexed, and had sex with all his leading ladies, but they have all said it did not happen, that was part of the image Parker put out there, but it was not Elvis.

Some have wrongly stated he could not or did not have sex because of his medication in the 70s, this is also untrue, as many of his girlfriends in the 70s have attested to. Elvis would rather just kiss and cuddle and read and sing to his girlfriends whatever his age was, until he was absolutely sure about the other person.

There are many videos of his early girlfriends on YouTube saying they never had sex long before he took any medications, Elvis did not believe in sex before marriage, even Cilla will attest to that. Elvis never wanted to just have sex with anyone, he was looking for that someone special he had a connection with. Had Elvis ever found that one person he felt a spiritual connection to on this physical plane of existence, (which sadly he never did) the one who could fill that hole in his heart and give him inner peace then their lovemaking would have been a sacred spiritual act, two souls entwining together, not the sex he was expected to perform by so many and never did, for him that was emptiness and not worth the effort. Elvis even wanted to become a Buddhist Monk in the 60s if he was as sex-crazed as some think he would not have wanted to, but Cilla and Parker talked him out of it because they did not want to lose their cash cow, he even announced he was going to become celibate one time in the mid to late 60s. It is about time people forgot the hype and realised who Elvis the man was, he was NOT the image manufactured for him.

Even Cilla has admitted that Elvis was not interested in sex and did not do it with his leading ladies, like we have been led to believe.

Some people say Elvis was humble, that he was shy, what it was is he had low self-esteem, a fragile ego, he never thought himself good enough, and this manifested itself in many ways.

He always bit his fingernails, he chewed gum and smoked, though rarely inhaled, in an effort not to bite his fingernails but it did not work, he was nearly always nervous, and he could not take criticism it cut him to his very soul, which is why he always did everything he did to his best ability. He always gave 100% in whatever he was doing, whether on stage singing or recording, it had to be perfect no matter how many takes it took. It is the same reason he hated doing some of the movies so much it made him physically ill, because he knew no matter how good he was in them, the movies themselves were not good. When Elvis looked in a mirror it was not because he was being vain or a narcist like some might tell you, it was because he was making sure he looked good so no one could criticize him.

Elvis was terrified of people not liking him, not loving him, that is why he gave so much of himself all the time, he needed people to love him with an overwhelming desire to try and fill that lonely hole he had in his heart which sadly he never did fully. It is why he let so many people use him because he hated being alone. Elvis had the greatest capacity for love and to love and be loved. Lisa was his greatest love. To Elvis children were almost sacred, he knew and understood how fragile they were and how easily their psyche could be damaged by thoughtless adults, as his had been by his mother. He was always especially gentle and acted kindly toward children making them feel like they mattered and were important to him, note how when you see a photo of him with a child he always bends down to their level, so they felt equal to him.

Elvis had the greatest relationship with his fans because they showed him that unconditional love he so needed, but he was still fearful they could turn against him which is why people like Parker could manipulate and control Elvis so easily. Parker learned early on about Elvis's daddy and uncle being in jail and he used the information like a whip against Elvis. Elvis was all too aware of how judgemental people were and that included, he thought, his fans, he never forgot the reactions of people toward him in the early days and how they burnt his effigy and called him the devil incarnate, and so a man who should of had all the confidence in the world had very little, and was always frightened that what he had achieved could be taken away from him in one fell swoop.

This is why he kept his spirituality and metaphysical beliefs closely guarded, he knew some of his public would not understand him believing in reincarnation, would not believe he was telepathic or practiced telekinesis or astral travel, yet all those who met him saw something superhuman about him, an undeniable aura of greatness, how sad he had to hide his real self from people for fear of ridicule, how much greater would his life have been if he had felt free to show people what he had mastered, yet even some of those he did show, the ones he called friends ridiculed him for it, how could they watch him control the weather and then laugh at him, it is no wonder he kept his secrets so hidden. Had Elvis of been born say in a place like India, he would have been a revered Yogi with his abilities, not hiding them for fear of ridicule.

Elvis was also an empath and felt other people's hurts and worries and was not afraid to show emotions and often would shed a tear with and for people, he was not afraid to cry like some men are, he was also a healer and there are many stories of him using his healing powers on his friends, and even since he died there are many stories of him helping people from spirit, a book has even been written about it. Elvis himself loved reading books all sorts and had a thirst for knowledge, he was an extremely intelligent man.

Red West said Elvis was a boy trapped in a man's body and in some ways that was true, he was very childlike in many ways, not childish, he had an innocence about him and he had a child's capacity for fun, he could find fun in anything, he hardly was ever still he had a lot of nervous energy and needed somewhere to channel it, he loved pillow fights and tickle fights, he loved going fast on anything, be it horses, motorbikes, cars or anything else, he loved karate and contrary to what some have said he was very good at it and gave it 100% like he did with everything. Elvis thought karate could benefit everyone, not just the athletic side to it but the meditation and ethos behind it. He also loved British humour like Peter Sellers Pink Panther and did a great impression of Inspector Clouseau, he also loved Monty Python and his irreverent Holy Grail movie, he also liked action movies like James Bond, science fiction ones, horror and supernatural and if a movie did not grab him in the first few minutes he would turn it off, sadly he did not get to see Star Wars, I have been told he was trying to get a copy when he died, I know he would have loved Yoda and I am sure would of impersonated him too and he would have totally got 'The Force', for the Force was in Elvis, it was how he saw the universe and god, not as a bearded Charlton Heston sitting on a cloud but as a Universal Force of love for everyone not held down by denominations or judgment of the different squabbling churches, Elvis knew of the gnostic gospels those that did not make the bible.

Elvis was a seeker of the truth, the Universal truth, he understood that time was not linear, he knew of the Akashic Record and what it holds, he could heal people with his touch and move things with his mind, he was the embodiment of love itself, as all those who ever went to one of his concerts knew and felt it and even those who never saw him in person still could and can feel that love he brought and gave so freely to all who wanted it. Elvis also believed in UFOs, and some would say he was a conspiracy nut, he was sure like many are that more than one person shot Kennedy and would watch it again and again trying to see the truth, the truth in all its shapes and forms was very important to Elvis.

Elvis hated being alone and surrounded himself with others and they were not always there because they were his true friends but some were his paid friends, yet even surrounded by people some he had known most of his life he always still felt alone, some think that was because he was a twin, some think because he was an old soul, many people who were not a twin have that longing and never find out why, for Elvis it could make life difficult and be a catch 22 situation, how could he have privacy when he hated to be alone, especially at sleep time, one of his entourage was always supposed to be with him or find someone else to be with him, (one of the reasons there are so many stories about Elvis having a different girl every night, he needed them for companionship, not what the press says) and check on him constantly partly because he had slept walked from an early age and his mother instilled on him and his friends he should not be left alone, one time when they found him sleep walking on a fire escape.

Some people will tell you he had a hair-trigger temper but that was because they did not understand him or how to say things to him, remember he had a very low self-esteem and low self-image, so when someone said 'no' to him or told him he could not do something he took it as a personal slight like he was not good enough or was stupid, so he retaliated because he was hurt by them, but his anger never lasted and he was always sorry afterwards when he understood, and of course some used it against him knowing they could get something as a sorry present.

Elvis always wanted to make people happy, it made him happy to spread joy, Elvis was the kindest, warmest most genuine person who made those around him feel like they were his best buddies even if they only knew him for two seconds because he knew how we all want to feel and that's how he made people feel, he made people feel like they were important to him.

Above all Elvis was a gentle man in every sense, who always thought of others needs even if they did not know it, as he said to his Daddy, 'you see their wants, I see their need', sadly a lot took advantage of that caring, giving spirit of his and did not return the love he gave, eventually even Elvis had to come to terms with it and recognise their disloyalty which was extremely hard for him, ironically I believe the book the Wests and Hebler wrote gave Elvis the courage to make those changes, though he never got the chance to put them in to practice, he had them planned. He wanted to go back to making movies, good ones, to fire Parker and others and stop the touring and Vegas, and most importantly he wanted full custody of Lisa. He knew if his fans still loved him after that book was released then nothing anyone said, Parker or anyone else would stop them loving him.

Elvis's most coveted dream was to bring the world together, had he been allowed to live I think he would have managed it. He matured a lot the last couple of years of his life and was overwhelmed when the then President Carter phoned him on New Year's eve 76/77 to ask him to be his 'special advisor for youth', and of course he excepted, sadly it never happened because that book happened instead, but had it happened, had he lived, I think he would have gone on to be an ambassador for world peace and he would have achieved his greatest dream, doors that would have been shut for most would have been opened for him because everyone wanted to meet him and his magnetism was so great that he could have achieved what no one else could, he could have and would made this world a better place, but those controlled by greed with hard hearts murdered him because he was worth more dead than alive. Had he lived today he might have been an elder statesman and I am sure still loved by all who met him.

CHARISMA

We know Elvis had it by the truckload, no one has the aura/charisma he did, as this person found out, and Elvis not only had the charisma, but he was a musical genius and self-taught extremely intelligent man with a vast knowledge of many things ancient and new. His charisma/aura/persona, call it what you will, was so magnetic, so electrifying that people said you could 'feel' him coming before he walked into a room, those fans who practically lived at the gates of his houses said you could 'feel' when he was home, it was so great.

"Sexual charisma, from the Greek 'kharisma', meaning 'gift from God', is an elusive and indefinable thing...a colleague at Stanford had once attempted the impossible task of defining it for his PhD thesis. He had interviewed scores of high-profile movie stars, politicians and successful businesspeople but discovered that although all had seemed attractive, magnetic, and charming, less than a handful had possessed genuine charisma in person. The rest were so disappointing he had abandoned his PhD. 'Essentially, charisma's as rare as genius,' he concluded..... Michael Cordy."

Exactly - we know that Elvis possessed not only genius but amazing charisma. The pundits are still trying to explain the Elvis charisma, without success. We of course know that it has no explanation but is felt by all who encountered him and continues down the years even though he is physically no longer with us!

SEXUAL URGES

I do not know when Elvis said this and cannot verify it, but from what I know of Elvis it is how he felt. "I feel that if you can't control sex - the physical impulse for sex - then you can't control anything in your life. You cannot let your body - its desires - rule you. It cannot master your mind, your heart. If you allow it, then all is lost. Sure, I have desires... but by damn, I am the master of my body. I am the deciding factor and I rule. The day comes that I can't then I'm dead. There is more to life than flexing muscle and I intend to follow a code of honour in my life - that's important. My self-esteem, my feelings of self-worth and living with my heart and conscience. Life is too short to waste it in vain regrets".

ELVIS ON CHILDREN

Elvis believed children were almost sacred, he said 'You know, if you look into your child's eyes and they look back at you, you can easily see what real trust is and it is scary, because they have such perfect love, without question and they have faith in you. It's a pity that so many parents don't take the time anymore to really look into their child's eyes'. Elvis said 'I figure all any child needs is hope and a feeling he or she belongs. If I could do or say anything that would give a child that feeling I would believe I had contributed something to the world'. Elvis knew making a child feel loved, wanted, and needed were the most important things you could give them, and to show them kindness and understanding so they could grow up to be good, compassionate adults.

ABORTION

I am sure Elvis's opinions about it were tempered when he lived as a child to teenager in Lauderdale Courts, he must have seen what not only women did to themselves in order to end a pregnancy but what happened to unwanted children that some had.

ELVIS ON ABORTION: -

"Abortion is so misunderstood. I believe women should cherish life - their ability to produce the living bodies that house Spirits - but if they cannot handle the reproductive process, then why force them to do so? I do not see the reason behind that." Also remember when Cilla told him she was pregnant Elvis asked her if she wanted an abortion, so although he loved Lisa more than anything once she was born, he did not want to force Cilla into having a child she did not want, Elvis would have loved more children, but Cilla made it plain that she did not want any more children with him.

ELVIS TALKS ABOUT REINCARNATION

Elvis was a firm believer in reincarnation and although I do not have the source for this quote, I have no doubt it is real as he said similar things about his ex-wife to several of his girlfriends. Elvis talks about Priscilla.

"I just realized why my first attraction to Priscilla happened— It's reincarnation. How else would a grown man be so drawn to a fourteen-year-old girl? Man....I used to think she was my soulmate. Now I know she wasn't the one; at least, not my soulmate. She was only a dress rehearsal and not the real thing. It must be some sort of karma we obviously had together, only I'm sure it's all from another life and another time."

"I tried to mould her into what I thought I wanted. I realized too late that you just can't do that. You can't teach a person to be affectionate. By nature, she's a cold person. She's reserved. She's very disciplined. Very reserved. Very cold. So, I tried to teach her to be warm, funny, loving, and affectionate. She tried to do it, but you really can't teach someone to be what they aren't."

ELVIS DID NOT WANT TO MARRY CILLA, HERE HIS COOK TELLS HER STORY

One day before Elvis married Priscila, his housekeeper and cook Alberta Holman caught him crying in despair, about the upcoming wedding, and she asked him what was wrong, and Elvis replied "I don't want to marry Priscilla". And she asked Elvis why he didn't just cancel it if it was making him so unhappy" but Elvis said "I can't, I have no choice" (claims suggested Priscilla had pressured Elvis into marriage, threatening to go to the press with the details about their relationship, especially when she was 14 and 15 years old).

Source - All Shook Up - Elvis Day By Day - Lee Cotten (1998), it is also in Down at the End of Lonely Street: The Life and Death of Elvis Presley by Peter Harry Brown and Pat H. Broeske

ELVIS COULD FLY HIS JET

Elvis was not the sort of man to just give up, as I have said he had plans for his future, I honestly think he knew what might happen to him if he trod on to many of the wrong toes as he told by Larry Geller in his book 'If I Can Dream' about Elvis being owned by the mob, I think this is why he had learned to fly his jet and not told anyone officially, though from time to time he did take controls of the jet, not just to fly it in the air but to land it too, now flying a jet in the air even taking off is nowhere near as difficult as landing a jet, yet Elvis did it, so I believe he did have flying lessons in secret to be able to do this.

This is testimony from Lisa about Elvis flying and landing the jet, now Lisa makes it sound like hijinks here but landing a jet full of people, people you love is not something you do unless you KNOW you can do it.

"Apparently Elvis occasionally liked to land his private jet as well, another opportunity for friends and family to fear for their lives. "Same with the plane. All of a sudden, the captain would come on, saying 'please fasten your seatbelts,' because [Elvis] was going to land the plane. It was just like everybody would stick their head between their knees and hide or something… bury themselves in their seats. It was just one of those 'Oh good God' moments."

Remember Elvis insured his jet to fly to both Britain and Japan in 1976, I think it was part of his escape plan, if he had got word he was about to be murdered he would have simply gathered all his family on to his plane and took off, sadly he never got that chance, but I sincerely think it was part of his forward planning why else do it when he knew he would never be allowed to leave America by Parker or the mob, that they would never allow him out of their control and we all know Parker could not leave America as he was an illegal immigrant.

Insurance certificate proving Elvis had every intention of coming to England and Japan

AVIATION QUESTIONNAIRE

AMERICAN EAGLE LIFE INSURANCE COMPANY
Newark, New Jersey

1. Name of proposed insured (Please Print)
   First — Elvis   Middle — Aaron   Last — Presley

2. Have you ever flown as a pilot, student pilot, or crew member or do you intend to do so? Yes [X] No [ ]
   If yes complete 3, 4, 5, 6, 7 and 8.

3. NUMBER OF HOURS FLOWN AS

	CIVILIAN							MILITARY			
	COMMERCIAL				NON-COMMERCIAL						
	PAST 12 mos.	ESTIMATED NEXT 12 mos.	TOTAL TO DATE	DATE OF LAST FLIGHT	PAST 12 mos.	ESTIMATED NEXT 12 mos.	TOTAL TO DATE	DATE OF LAST FLIGHT	PAST 12 mos.	ESTIMATED NEXT 12 mos.	TOTAL TO DATE	DATE OF LAST FLIGHT
PILOT OR CO-PILOT												
STUDENT PILOT												
CREW MEMBER					20	25	45					

4. If you have flown as a civilian, complete this additional information.
   4a. Type of Plane ....
   b. Type of airman certificate held ....
   c. In what capacity? ....
   d. Owner of Plane ....
   e. Do you own a plane or intend to own a plane ....

5. If you have flown in the Military services, complete this additional information.
   5a. Type of plane ....
   b. Rank or rate ....
   c. Reserve or regular? ....
   d. Active or inactive? ....
   e. Pilot Classification ....

6. Have you been involved in any accident resulting in injury to any person, or requiring reinspection of any aircraft? Yes [ ] No [X]
   6a. Explain fully here ....

7. Do you intend to fly outside continental United States or Canada? Yes [X] No [ ]
   7a. What countries? Japan & England
   b. Routes ....
   c. Base ....

8. Have you ever engaged in, or do you contemplate engaging in Jet Plane Flying, Student Instruction, Stunt Flying, Crop Dusting, Test or experimental flying, or Racing? Yes [ ] No [X]
   8a. Explain fully here ....

9. Have you flown within two years as a passenger, except on regularly scheduled commercial airlines, or do you intend to do so? Yes [X] No [ ]
   Full time crew
   X-TWA pilot, co-pilot & engineer, pilot & co-pilot experience over 15,000 hours plus.
   9a. Purpose of flights Pleasure & business
   b. Over what routes or areas are flights made? U.S.
   c. Experience of pilots (3) TWA Pilots
   d. Service facilities available ....
   e. Type of plane Convair 880
   f. Owner of plane self
   g. Flight hours, past 12 months 20 estimated next 12 months 25 total to date 45 date of last flight Current

10. Have you flown within the last year as a passenger on regular scheduled airlines, or do you intend to do so? Yes [ ] No [X]
    10a. Total number of hours past year ....
    b. Total hours estimated next year 50

I hereby declare that all the statements and answers to the above questions are complete and true, and I agree that they shall form a part of my application for insurance dated *August 11, 1976*, and become a part of any contract of insurance issued on such application.

Dated at *Memphis, Tenn.* this *11* day of *August* 19*76*

_____ Witness   X _____ Sign name in full   Proposed Insured

[30]

THE TRIBE OF DAN

This ring is from Elvis, it's very heavy, made from metal, not silver, not all gold and seems to be brass and something? It is big. On the sides are shields with the three-point top and oval/rounded sides and bottom. On the shields that can still be seen somewhat, it's very well worn and old, are eagles with the wings spread and the head sideways-they are small, and they are standing on big boughs it looks like, though

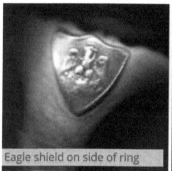
Eagle shield on side of ring

Top of ring

hard to tell it's so worn. There is a blue inlay of some kind below the bough and rounded areas that seem to be water maybe or perhaps clouds in the sky? Above the eagle's head is a curved long vine or something with one arrowhead looking leaf at the end? that's on the sides of the ring. The top has a large base that is bevelled to look like, sun rays all around a centre that has a raised bed of what looks like copper, and on top of that is another "set" that is about 1/2 inch long and a tad less wide with a cut off top and bottom to the whole thing. Now, in the centre of the top setting is some kind of design that has gold set into it or onto it in the very centre-when the light or sun hits it is sends a bright light out of it. The top is a rough cross it is worn down too, and there is behind the cross red colour inlay. Across the whole bed is some white inlay that looks like maybe a robe-or part of one-it's worn down too. And at the bottom is about 4 curved narrow blue inlays. Now, the entire set with the colour and markings is edged in gold. Around the under bed is a wreath of leaves that go all around the top setting of metal and coloured areas. It has religious meanings in some way-spiritual meanings of some type. The entire thing is strange as it was very old and handmade-roughly hand-made but extremely well detailed I imagine when new. This ring was given to Elvis, he was supposed to give it back when he did not complete the necessary steps and etc: that it took to reach his goal to be a priest so he could really help people in need of spiritual guidance. This was when Elvis was wearing those big scarves over his shoulders-different colours-white for step one, gold for step two and there was two more-with the last one to be lavender.

He gave it up because Priscilla (even though they were separated and divorcing) ridiculed his efforts and desires so much, and convinced him he was not able to handle his own problems-how could he even think he could handle anyone else's? etc. Anyway, Elvis felt he could not do it-plus he could not rid himself of the sleeping pills entirely at that time either. He thought they were wrong for what he wanted to be and do also. This ring was supposed to be more than one hundred years old -They would not take it back from him because they felt he should have it-he was very moved by that...Elvis did not tell much, just that it was old and that it carried within it all the "saints" who had gone before, given their life for their religious beliefs and to save mankind from evil and that it belonged to the master priest-which he was striving to become one of. They gave it to Elvis at his second ceremony and he was to take full charge of all it meant at the 4th, but he never completed the 3 or 4th-and they wouldn't take it back as It "belonged with him" the headmaster told him. He ought to have it. But to wear it sparingly as he had not fulfilled his full training and it was "powerful". Elvis said it was the only one, the original handmade and designed by those who formed the society of the brotherhood. He would not say who, what or where. He did not want to talk about it.

Elvis wearing two of the different coloured scarves associated with when he was doing the Tribe of Dan.

Elvis Presley's Employment History

The summer of Elvis' freshman year of high school, his dad Vernon bought him a push lawn mower. With the mower and a couple of sickles, Elvis and his three buddies - Buzzy Forbes, Farley Guy and Paul Dougher - started a lawn business. They charged $4.00 per yard. This was the beginning of the working life a young man who would very soon become a millionaire.

Elvis received his Social Security card # 409-52-2002 in September 1950. He then went to work as an usher at Loew's State Theatre on Main Street in Memphis.

Starting in June 1951, Elvis held a summer job at Precision Tool. He worked three months operating a spindle drill press at this plant, which manufactured rocket shells for the military. He made $27.00 a week. That same year he took his driver's license test using his uncle Travis Smith's 1940 Buick.

In April 1952 Elvis returned to Loew's State Theatre as an usher, only to be fired five weeks later for an altercation with a fellow usher. Some say it was started by the other usher, prompted by his jealousy over a female employee's apparent fondness for Elvis. Soon after, in June, Vernon Presley bought a 1941 Lincoln, which became regarded as Elvis' car. It is said he spent more time pushing it than driving it.

In August 1952 Elvis applied at the Upholsterers Specialties Company. On the application he gave his date of birth as January 8, 1934, adding a year to his stated age in order to qualify as old enough to work there. He worked there one month, earning $109.00.

In September 1952 Elvis worked for MARL Metal Products, a furniture manufacturer. He worked the 3:00 PM - 11:00 PM shift as an assembler. His mother Gladys made him quit this job because he kept falling asleep in school.

On March 26, 1953, Elvis visited the Tennessee State Employment Security Office. On his application he wrote under 'leisure time activities': 'Sings, playing ball, working on car, going to movies'. The interviewer noted: 'rather flashily dressed 'playboy' type'.

On April 6, 1953, he visited the employment office again and updated his application for work saying he wanted to operate 'big lathes'. On another visit to the employment office on July 1, 1953, Elvis reported he needed to 'work off financial obligations and that he owns his own automobile'. This time he was sent to the M. B. Parker Company for a temporary job as an assembler. He worked there until the job ran out at the end of the month, making 90-cents an hour or $36.00 a week.

Returning to the employment office in August 1953, he indicated he wanted a job in which he could 'keep clean'. He was sent to several places for interviews, including a Sears & Roebuck store and a Kroger grocery store. He was not hired from any of these interviews.

On September 21, 1953, Elvis returned to Precision Tool company, operating a drill press for $1.55 an hour. He continued to work there until March 19, 1954. Elvis filed his first income tax return on March 6, 1954, listing himself as 'semi-skilled labour' and having earned at total of $129.74 at M.B. Parker and $786.59 at Precision Tool for a total of $916.33.

On April 20, 1954, Elvis began working at Crown Electric for $1.00 an hour. He delivered supplies to the job sites and hoped to train to be an electrician. He stayed at Crown until mid-October 1954 after officially become a self-employed entertainer having recorded his first record at Sun Studio. In 1955, he reported on his income tax return a total of $25,240.15 in earnings. This figure would jump the following year to $282,349.66.

By 1958 he had earned over a million dollars in one year. In a short time, he had come a long way from his days behind a push mower.

THE GIVER

Most know about Elvis giving to just about everyone he met when he was famous, and I have even heard some naysayers saying it wasn't anything special cause he had all that money why should he not give some to others. The truth is Elvis was always a giver it was his nature to give, it always had been, here are two stories that Vernon talked about Elvis as a child.

When Elvis was young they didn't have much and what they did have went on necessities like food, but sometimes they would have a little leftover and would spend it on their young son and buy him a toy, but to their dismay Elvis would nearly always give it away, Vernon said at first they were angry at Elvis for doing this, they had worked hard for the money to buy him something and thought he was being ungrateful

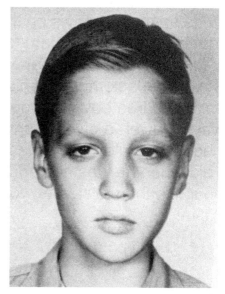

giving it away, but Vernon said he soon realised that the young Elvis was not being ungrateful when Elvis told them that he had given his toys to someone who had less than him, and Vernon was proud of his boy for being so charitable.

Now in those days in America sadly racism was still very much in play (from both sides I might add as Elvis would find out when he tried to break into the music business), segregation was still the norm and whites and coloureds did not mix, at least not in public. On one hot steamy southern summers day Vernon bought his young son a special treat, an ice cream cone, Elvis sat down on the sidewalk/path to eat it, as he started to eat it he saw this young coloured boy about his age coming towards him, you could practically see him drooling at the sight of the ice cream, so as he passed Elvis asked him if he wanted a lick, of course the young boy said yes and he sat next to Elvis on the sidewalk curb and they ate the ice cream together, sharing it lick for lick, something that would be virtually unheard of back then, a white boy eating food with a coloured boy. So, you see Elvis was always a giver, a giver to anyone who he thought he could help, it was not just something he did when he was rich and famous to gain favour like the naysayers would have you believe.

DRAFTED AND SHAFTED

Elvis rarely made his personal views public which is why so many have the wrong impression of how he felt about things and being drafted is one of them. Think about it why would he want to be drafted he was on the crest of a wave with his career, the world at his feet, why would he want to give all that up, of course he would not, His cousin Junior had come back from Korea a broken and changed man from his days of being drafted and eventually killed himself, so Elvis had plenty of reasons not to go. His mother was critically ill, and he expected Parker to get him out of the draft, which he could have easily done, given that Elvis was an only child, his mother being critically ill and with him being the breadwinner not only for his immediate family but also his extended family. I dare say a lot of people's livelihoods in Memphis depended on Elvis not being drafted, but Parker had other ideas, Parker wanted to get rid of Elvis's bad-boy rebel image and wanted to make him more wholesome, indeed some have even said Elvis being drafted was a fix, Parker got a stay for him being called up so he could finish filming King Creole. Elvis received his callup papers just before that Christmas of 57 and he was furious, so furious his words are reported to have been, 'They want war I'll give them war', and he bought up every available firework he could in Tennessee and surrounding states and the first war game was had, which later became a tradition.

Many might not believe this but it is true, don't forget that one of Elvis's best friends and real true friends was Muhammad Ali, who would not abide by the draft, now that alone should prove to you Elvis also did not agree with the draft and do not forget one of Elvis's cousins was never the same after he came back from Korea and died an early death, and if Elvis had not of been drafted his mother would have lived longer and Cilla would have never met Elvis, in fact had Parker not had his draft put off till he finished the movie he would have not met Cilla or Joe, the two people who I believe were Elvis's downfall along with Parker.

Charlie tells the story in his book. Elvis was out on manoeuvres with his senior officer next to the border in sub-zero temperatures, where they should not have been, when night-time came, they fell asleep with the engine running. Elvis woke just in time, feeling sick, he fell out of the jeep and threw up and then noticed his officer was already unconscious, Elvis dragged him out of the jeep into the fresh air, another minute or two and both could have been beyond saving, and possibly their bodies never recovered, so please think about it, would Elvis being drafted have been worth it if he had died.

GLADYS AND ELVIS

I know some are not going to like this, but I think
it is crucial in understanding who Elvis was.
A lot of people ask why did Elvis not fire Parker,
why did Elvis let Parker get away with so much,
why did Elvis let Cilla be so horrible to him, why
Elvis did not stick up for himself, why did he let
his so-called friends walk all over him, this is
why. I know a lot of people think Gladys could
do no wrong, I know a lot of people will not like
what I have to say but to deny the effect she had
on Elvis is doing both a disservice.

Gladys had a very hard upbringing, she had to
look her mother and all her siblings and father.
Her mother took to her bed, and it was left to
Gladys to look after everyone, her mother was
supposed to have consumption, but she had
approximately nine children including Gladys, so
there was not that much wrong with her, and she
lived to almost 60 yrs. old. Gladys had been
brought up to be very god-fearing, fearing many
things with very strong morals as well. She was
a product of her upbringing and I in no way am
blaming her, but the way she was with Elvis did
not help him. Elvis had more wisdom and
empathy at a young age than a lot of adults do,
he knew his mamma had problems and did not
blame her for them, if anything like a lot of
children he possibly blamed himself for making
her angry, it is that that made him into what they
call a 'people pleaser'. Could Vernon had done

something to stop her, possibly, but mental health was not very well looked at in those days.

When Gladys was happy everyone was happy and when she wasn't no one was. Gladys had always had a hair-trigger temper and there is a story of her almost killing a man when she was about twelve. I am sure after losing Jesse she probably had post-natal depression which would have exacerbated her behaviour. Then Vernon going to prison and losing the house would have just added to it. Elvis took the brunt of her anger, but as you will see in a story further down, it wasn't his pain that concerned him but his mothers. Even when she was beating him, he knew she loved him and that was all that mattered to Elvis. To begin with, Gladys was desperate to get married and get away from looking after her family, she was getting older and was possibly frightened of being left on the shelf. She tried to elope with a man before she met Vernon, but it did not happen. Then she met Vernon, they had only known each other a short while before she talked him into eloping with her. Vernon was not much more than a boy at 17 and I am sure he was enthralled by this older woman, plus it gave him a status of manhood, and he probably thought his father would not look down at him anymore - Jesse was not a good father or husband. They had to go across state borders to get married because Vernon was too young to get married and she also lied about her age saying she was younger than she was.

Gladys fell pregnant and when a car ran into the side of their car, on Gladys's side, Vernon used the money to build a house next to his parents' house, not the Smith's. I believe it was this crash that was the cause of Jesse being stillborn. So why would she tell a small child that he was a twin and let him believe it was his fault his twin died, why even tell Elvis about his dead twin at all? A mother is supposed to protect her child from hurt not exacerbate it. I am sure Gladys was suffering from post-natal depression especially with losing one of her babies, and like most women when their child dies for whatever reason they feel guilty - and I am sure the fact Gladys's mother died the same year, only made her worse and feel even more guilty. Still, a good mother is not supposed to put that guilt onto their living child.

When young Elvis would talk to his dead brother, he got into trouble for that too, how else was this small child supposed to handle the fact he had a dead brother, and it was his fault. When Gladys caught him doing it, she would wash his mouth out with soap and water, telling him that it was the devil's work when people heard voices. It is hard enough for adults to grasp the consequences of death - how is a small child supposed to.

When Vernon was jailed for changing the amount on a cheque, Gladys did not protect the three-year-old Elvis from it. She did not tell him Daddy was working away and we can go and see him - no, she sat on her porch wailing and telling Elvis he had to be the man of the family cause daddy was in jail, just to get sympathy from the neighbours. So, they petitioned the governor of the jail to get Vernon out early and it worked but at what cost to the three-yr. old Elvis who felt responsible for his mother and father. Most people have no recognition of being three years olds, but Elvis had this second huge burden put on his shoulders.

When Elvis was four and still trying to be the man of the house, a neighbour took pity on him and gave him some empty cola bottles so he could return them to get the pennies. Gladys with her high moral standards decided this was stealing, even though the neighbour had given the bottles to Elvis. She had Vernon take a switch to him and if that wasn't bad enough, she then shamed him in front of everyone in the church - making him stand there with a sign around his neck saying he was a thief, at four years old, can you imagine what that did to a four-year-old. Later in Elvis's own words, after he had won a singing contest, he went home to tell his mother and she 'whooped the ego right out of him', and he laughs embarrassingly when he says it. He could not remember exactly what the beating was for, most children who get beaten often never know what the beating is for.

For Elvis, being beat by his mother was an everyday occurrence, to Gladys with her old-fashioned morals, pride and ego were sins that had to be beaten out of you. Yes, she also showered him with love to, but it had a cost, he had to be good to get it. He could not be who he wanted to be but who she wanted him to be - Elvis exhibited every sign of an abused child. Gladys could be extremely sweet but also brutal, she was the one in charge in that house and Vernon and Elvis did as they were told. It has been said you never heard Vernon raise his voice, it was always Gladys. One time she hit Vernon that hard with a pan she not only knocked him out of the chair he was sitting in but knocked him unconscious.

The fact neither of them could cope after she died, is another sign, they had been told what to do for so long they could not make their own decisions, which is why Vernon married the first woman who came along to tell him what to do. It is the same reason why Elvis made such bad choices with his girlfriends and let Cilla do whatever she wanted and treat him like dirt, as long as she stayed. And why he let Parker get away with whatever he wanted to do, because Elvis was unable to stand up for himself - because he had such a low opinion of himself, low self-esteem, and no confidence in his ability.

Even though he had millions of adoring fans he was terrified of not being liked, let alone loved, it is why he paid friends to be with him.

Do not think of Gladys as a poor little woman It is said that this little woman one time had Red West cornered against a wall with a knife to his throat and told him she would kill him if he let anything happen to her boy. She was a determined woman and Elvis lived for her, would have done anything for her - but he could not stand up for himself, because he thought he was not worthy. If Gladys had been different, if she had encouraged Elvis to be proud of himself, to have the confidence to make his own decisions - his life would have been completely different. Even the pent-up rage and the blaming himself and not being able to express it all, point to an abused child. Gladys did what she thought was best for her son and I do not blame her, but you have to understand the relationship to understand why Elvis was who he was. Why he allowed people to walk all over him, why he made such bad choices in 'friends' and girlfriends, why he rarely stood up for himself against people. Because he was never allowed to, as a child or teenager, so he never learned how to do it because Gladys always made the decisions for him. Without her he was lost, she did not bring him up to be independent of her but to depend on her.

Elvis became famous because he wanted to do something good for his mother, buy her all the things she never had. You would think this would make her happy and she would be grateful to Elvis for all his hard work, she was not, she actually said she wished she was poor again. When he was on the road touring in the early days, he would phone his baby every night, his baby was not his girlfriend - it was Gladys. He knew if she was talking to Elvis she wouldn't be fighting with Vernon. When his actual girlfriend got tired of waiting for him it was Gladys who told Elvis he had been dumped, but even then, Gladys was not happy with Elvis, for she could see him becoming more independent of her and she did not like it. When one time she went to one of his concerts and Elvis became excited on stage, as often happened, Gladys made a show of him in front of everyone who was there backstage waiting for him, because he had an erection, imagine how he felt, he never asked Gladys to go to a concert again. Gladys did not like Elvis being famous, she did not like the fact she was losing control over Elvis and someone else had that control.

Gladys didn't like the fact Elvis was becoming famous and having friends in Hollywood, so when Elvis took Natalie Wood home to meet his mamma, she told Elvis to come sit on his mammas lap. That was all the sign that Natalie needed to know Elvis was possessed and controlled by Gladys, she had her mom phone saying there was a family emergency and she had to go back to LA. Gladys got her way once again. She never allowed Elvis to grow up, it is why people he knew would say he was a child in a man's body.

Gladys also didn't like the fact she was losing control to Parker. When Elvis phoned his Mamma from the set of "Jail House Rock" upset because Parker was making a fool of him and laughing at his family with the film (by this time Parker knew that Elvis' father and uncle had been to jail) Gladys told Elvis to do whatever Parker wanted him to do so the

shame of the family would not be leaked to the press by Parker. Once again putting tremendous pressure on Elvis. If she had told Elvis to tell Parker where to shove it, he would have done, but once again he was not allowed to do what he thought was right. He had to bow to others wishes and let himself be made a fool of in his eyes. Imagine how empowering it would have been for Elvis if he had been allowed to tell Parker where to go, but right there the seal was set.

Gladys, was losing her grip on Elvis, and she started drinking heavily and when Elvis got drafted, she could not bear it, and the fact it was put off till he finished filming King Creole made it even worse, it gave her time to get even more upset and drink heavily, so instead of happily waving her son off to give him happiness she was visibly grief-stricken, making Elvis feel even more guilty. She then drunk so heavily so got hepatitis and her heart gave out, she had drunk herself into an early grave and once again Elvis felt he was to blame. The burden she put on his shoulders because of her selfishness was unimaginable - when all he ever did was try to make her happy and proud. When people were asked about Gladys - often the first thing they say is how possessive and controlling of Elvis Gladys was.

When he went to school, she would follow him to make sure he went and that he did not get into any trouble on the way. She even made him take his own cutlery to school to use,

we can only imagine how the other pupils reacted to this sort of things. It is no wonder Elvis had few friends in school and was constantly bullied. When Elvis was seven years old his daddy took him to the movies, something that was banned and said to be sinful by the church that Gladys went to - in fact it has been said that everything that made you happy as far as that church was concerned was the devil's work. So, Vernon had to take Elvis there in secret because if Gladys ever found out both of them would be in trouble. The movie was a comedy and when Elvis came out of the theatre, he knew that the church was wrong. At that tender age of seven, already he was wiser than many adults. Elvis knew his mother had problems and never blamed her for the way she treated him.

This is in a book from his neighbour in Tupelo who used to look after Elvis while Gladys was at work (As a small boy) "Elvis used to sneak off from home to go to a creek that had a small cove with still water. And he went there to pray and to talk to Jesus, he said. He also said he talked to the 'angels' on the water and they sang to him. He told his mother when she came and caught him, and she said he was evil, doing evil things and whipped him. She also spanked his hands with a board once because he was 'using devil sign language' (hand signals of some kind). Elvis was small, yet he didn't cry even though she hit his hands until they were bright red. He told her when she started crying, 'It's okay Momma, you don't understand, It's okay.' Then he cried too and hugged her.

Elvis also liked to sit in the moonlight and stare at the sky, but when asked what he was doing he would say, 'getting moonbeams in my heart'. He said he could hear music in the heavens - beautiful singing, angels on high. His mother told him never to tell people because they would say he was evil, crazy, and lock him up. And his grandmother said Gladys often washed his mouth with soap when he did talk about hearing voices and seeing things. So, Elvis learned to keep quiet, and only told a few who understood about people with 'the gift' as Mary called it. Elvis, she said, had 'the gift' and had it in abundance. She told him to treasure it, that it was God talking to him. He hugged her and said, 'Thank you Mrs. Jones, I know.' He'd say to her, 'Someday, I'm going to tell people all about God and they'll listen to me! I'm going to make them listen to me all over the world!' and they did - he reached the world with his singing gospel. Mary said that one day Elvis was crying, and she asked him what was wrong. He said, 'Mrs. Jones, I got nobody to talk to and I need to so bad.' She said to him. 'Talk to your Momma', and he said, 'Mrs. Jones, my momma don't understand - I can't explain - she just gets upset and I can't upset her with this. I got nobody and I'm scared that no one will ever understand. Do you know, Mrs. Jones, what it is to be all alone in a place that is not ever going to be your home? I am going to be there - and I got nobody to understand.' And he cried until he shook.

I believe Linda Thompsons has said this story is one of the many reasons Elvis was very insecure: - "One day when we were sitting together in bed, as we usually were when we were relaxing, he told me a secret that made me love the little boy he'd been, the little boy who got bullied at school, the little boy who grew up in the Memphis version of the ghetto. "Mommy, you know these high-collared outfits, and shirts and suits that I wear?" "Yes, honey," I said. "Before I was able to have those kinds of clothes made for me, I would always turn my collar up." "Yes, I remember," I said, thinking back to the mesmerizing photos of him early in his career, which I'd admired in fan magazines long before he'd become my love. "Everybody thinks I did that because I think I'm cool," he said. "It's really because when I was a little shaver, and I was sitting at the kitchen table, my mama and daddy used to come by and say, 'Look at that little chicken neck. Look at that little scrawny neck.'" "Aw, honey," I said, putting my arms around him, even as I couldn't help but giggle compassionately. "So I was always self-conscious about my neck," he said. "I thought I had a skinny little chicken neck, because my mama and daddy said that to me when I was little, sitting at the kitchen table. That's why I've always worn my collar turned up. It's not because I think I'm cool, or I'm trying to be cool. It's because I'm trying to hide my little chicken neck. The people don't understand that. But you know because I'm telling you."

Linda wasn't the only girlfriend in the 70s Elvis talked to about his mother beating/whooping him, he told other girlfriends to who I have spoken to, which to me tells me he was finally realising what his childhood and mother had done to him, and he was facing up to it and wanting people to know, which is a huge step for any battered child. Someone once told me the reason he was frightened of the dark was because Gladys would also shut him in a cupboard, but I have never been able to verify this story, so I do not know if it is true or not, but it has been written in other books he never slept in the dark, he always had a light on.

The real tragedy is that Elvis was only just beginning to realise who he really was and to stand up for himself when he died, what a totally different life he could have had if his mother had not been so controlling. How great could he have become, as a singer and as an actor, or even a Buddhist monk like he wanted to in the 60s. His whole life he did things because it was what other people wanted, never what he wanted. All he ever tried to do was make people happy so they would like him and love him, and what he never got from hardly anyone was respect. How could he, when he did not know how to respect himself, as his TCB oath shows. The first line of which reads, 'More self-respect'. Many people have said that Elvis was like a child trapped in a man's body, some found that side of him fun and endearing, but the other side of that was that some thought he lacked impulse control, if he wanted to do something he wanted to do it now, like when he took Lisa to find snow in his jet, Elvis could do that cause he had that kind of money, and because he had such a giving nature, it meant he really did not have much money left, now I know most will not agree with me but this for me just clarifies even more the destructive nature Gladys had on Elvis and who he was and how difficult he found it to be normal. He could not bear to make a scene and so because of his inability to confront people he allowed them to walk all over him.

Anyone who comes from a violent home, as Elvis did, knows how this feels. "What causes poor impulse control? When children are raised in families where violence, verbal abuse, emotional abuse, physical abuse, and explosive emotional reactions to certain situations are prevalent, they may be at a higher risk for developing some type of impulse control disorder."
I personally think it is a testament to Elvis's innate goodness that he did not end up being totally anti-social, most murderers have a bad childhood like Elvis did and yet he was as kind and thoughtful as anyone could wish someone to be. (I have qualifications in counselling and psychology)

http://www.iheartelvis.net/tag/i-heart-elvis

Blue Star Love: From an Amazing Heart of Grace book by Maia Chrystine Nartoomid

Elvis and Gladys by Elaine Dundy

https://www.youtube.com/watch?v=XtuWKqfUzU
E&t=5s

ELVIS'S FAMILY TREE AND HEALTH HISTORY/LONGEVITY

You can see here that most of his relatives lived long lives for that time including Gladys's mother. I have heard a lot of people say that Elvis was extremely ill because had bad genes, this is nonsense, they say that because his mother died in her forties that it was obvious Elvis would too, but this is rubbish, Elvis's mother died because she was an alcoholic and had hepatitis and was heartbroken that Elvis had to go into the army and her heart gave out, but it was not because she had a bad heart to begin with and neither did Elvis, the official report said his heart stopped but they could not find out why, there is no indication that any of Elvis's relative died early in fact the opposite is true as you can see below

Elvis had acute constipation which he had since a child and passed on to Lisa, and on occasion a twisted colon, he also had viral arthritis which possibly caused the glaucoma and he suffered from insomnia and migraines, he also had sleepwalked since a child, but none of Elvis's ailments were life-threatening.

Elvis's double cousin Patsy, (double because her father is Vester, Vernon's brother, and her mother is Gladys's sister) is still alive and her genes would be the closest to Elvis's. His grandmother Minnie Mae lived till she was just short of her 90th birthday, Elvis's father Vernon was 63 but he was a heavy smoker, Gladys's mother even though she is said to of had 'consumption' lived to be 59 and had 9 children which to me means she had a very strong constitution to have that many children and live that long and having 'consumption' for years.

Daughter of Robert Lee Smith and Octavia Lavenia "Doll" Smith

Octavia Luvenia Smith (born Mansell) was born in May 1876, in Mississippi, to Albert White Mansell and Martha Mansell (born Tackett).

Albert was born in 1849, in Hamilton, Marion, Alabama, USA.

Martha was born in 1853, in Saltillo, Itawamba, Mississippi, USA.

Octavia had 5 siblings: Melissa Mansell, Jehru Mansell and 3 other siblings.

Octavia married Robert Lee Smith on the 30 September 1903, in Mississippi.

Robert was born in 1876, in Saltillo, Lee County, Mississippi.

They had 9 children: Effie Smith, Lillian Smith and 7 other children.
Octavia passed away in April 1935, at age 59.

"Minnie Mae Dodger Hood"

Birthdate: June 17, 1890 (89)

Birthplace: Fulton, Itawamba County, Mississippi.

Death: May 8, 1980 (89), Memphis, Shelby County, Tennessee, United States

Place of Burial: Memphis, Shelby County, Tennessee.

Daughter of William H. "Buck" Hood and Mary Louisa Hood

Ex-wife of Jessie D. McDowell Presley

Mother of Vester Presley; Delta Mae Biggs; Gladys Erlene Dowling; Rev Nashval Lorene Pritchitt; Calhoun Presley and Vernon Elvis Presley

Sister of Harrison Hood; Alice Hood; Minerva Hood; Sally Hood; William Hood and 2 others

Immediate Family:

Vernon Elvis Presley
Birthdate: April 10, 1916,
Birthplace: Fulton, Mississippi.
Death 26 June 1979.
He met and married Elvis's mother Gladys Smith when he was just 17. Gladys was four years older than him, and because Vernon was underage at the time, they lied about their ages in order to get married in 1933.

Gladys Love Presley (Smith)

Birthdate: April 25, 1912

Birthplace: Tupelo, Pontotoc, Mississippi, United States

Death: August 14, 1958 (46)

Methodist Hospital, Memphis, Shelby, TN, USA

Place of Burial: Memphis, Shelby County, Tennessee, United States

Wife of Vernon Elvis Presley. Mother of Jessie Garon Presley and Elvis Aaron Presley. Sister of Effie Smith; Lillian Mann Fortenberry; Lavell Smith; Retha Smith; Travis Smith and 7 others.

Occupation: Sewing Machinist, sewing machine operator.

Elvis gave most of the people he loved nicknames, it was just something he did if you were special to him.

This is Minnie Mae Presley, or Dodger as Elvis nicked named her, his grandmother.

VERNON ELVIS PRESLEY

Elvis's rock through all his later life was his father, his daddy, and you can see the love and pride they felt for each other in any photo of them together. Vernon often gets a bad rap from some people but how many know anything about Vernon, Gladys had already tried to elope once with another man, but it did not work out. Within weeks of meeting Vernon she took him across state lines because Vernon was not old enough to be legally married and married him lying about his age, he was just 17, Gladys was 4years old than him, when Gladys fell pregnant, Vernon was 18, he did not up and run like a lot of lads his age would have suddenly faced with this huge burden, no, what did this remarkable young man do, he built them a house with his bare hands, a house that still stands today, showing just how skilled he was at doing this task.

Did Vernon makes mistakes in his life of course he did, haven't we all, his biggest being altering a cheque/check he had been given in payment for a hog, urged on by Gladys's brother and another friend after they had been drinking, and what young man hasn't done something stupid when they feel they have been wronged when urged on to do so by their drinking buddies, but Vernon paid a heavy price for that mistake and ended up in jail, Vernon's father was not a good father to Vernon and paid for Gladys brother and their friends bail but left Vernon in jail, while he was there the land he had built their house on was sold by his father leaving Gladys and Elvis homeless and they went to live with Gladys's relatives, Vernon got let out of jail for good behaviour and being a hard worker early, but because he then had a record it meant afterwards work was hard to come by as it was for everyone in those years of the Great American Depression, but especially for someone who had spent time in jail, but he did his best by his family and took any job he could, one was on the docks where the fish was brought in and sold so they had a lot of fish to eat which is why Elvis hated the smell of fish in later life because it reminded him of his poor childhood, another one was a delivery driver which is when he hurt his back, (Elvis also suffered from a bad back and it caused him a lot of pain) but they stuck by each other through times so hard many could not imagine, and when you have lived through hard times of make do and mend with every penny counting it is hard to change which is why Elvis put his Daddy in charge of his finances, because he trusted him more than anyone. a good book to read about Elvis's early life is "Elvis and Gladys" by Elaine Dundy.

When Elvis was 7 years old his daddy Vernon took Elvis to the movies to see a comedy film, it had to be in secret because the religion and the church they went to was very strict and said that anything that was fun and gave you pleasure was a sin, and Gladys firmly believed this and would of had a fit had she known what Vernon had done with Elvis, but seeing that movie made Elvis realise that organised religion was wrong and things that gave you pleasure and made you happy were not a sin as he had been taught and that was when he made the first steps to becoming spiritual and not religious, to exploring everything there was to know about spirituality, had Vernon not done this, Elvis would never have become the person we know and love.

Everyone from childhood friends of Elvis's to his neighbours, to Dixie Locke, have all given interviews telling of anecdotes where Vernon was exhibiting behaviours of a traditional loving supportive father. Many of the black folks spoke very kindly of Vernon (including but not only) Elvis' childhood playmate Sam Bell. He pointed out how Vernon would remind Elvis to share his things and play nicely with the other kids, and Vernon also spent his time building a treehouse for Elvis so he and his playmates would all have that to enjoy. Elvis talked with Nick Adams about how his father took him to see the movie when he was a kid, they kept it from Gladys as their own little special memory and secret as mentioned above, a turning point in Elvis's life. Gladys herself in an interview spoke of how closely bonded Elvis was with his father when he was a child, he would worry about Vernon getting hurt.

Elvis even confided to Dixie Locke, and a couple of others, that before he was famous Vernon was a very supportive, sympathetic ear regarding what he should do about his future as a singer - telling Elvis that whatever he wanted to do he and his mother would support him. Vernon explained the music business was unpredictable, but if that was a route he wanted to go, he told Elvis to go for it, but he might also want to be prepared to think about a traditional trade or career. And that's when Elvis said he and his father discussed him studying to become an Electrician's Apprentice in case things didn't work out with Sun Records.

Vernon was also there defending Elvis in those early days in Memphis when some people were already saying bad things about Elvis. The Fruchters, the neighbours that the Presley's shared a building with, said often on many Saturdays they watched Elvis and Vernon waxing the family car together. As a close father and son would, spending a relaxing enjoyable bonding time together. The Tiplers, Elvis' bosses at Crown Electric company, said Vernon and Gladys both were there at the Eagles Nest in those first live gigs Elvis played... when the club was virtually empty. Contrary to mythology some of those first early gigs were not crowds flocking and gathering and jumping all around. They were literally big empty rooms, with only Scotty,

Bill and Elvis on the stage.... the staff working at the Eagles Nest... and his parents (and a couple of friends they brought with them to help cheer Elvis and the Blue Moon Boys on), and his mother and father were sitting at a table right there... always cheering him on. If Vernon was that against Elvis doing that .... that would have been his opportunity to point to Elvis and say "See! This is a big waste of time, and you won't be worth a damn, now get your rear end to that Electric company and get a real job", as so many seem to think, but Vernon did not. Vernon was always there for Elvis, always at his side backing him no matter what life threw at them, they were as close as a father and son could be. When Elvis was drafted and sent to Germany, before he had rented a house there and was still in barracks, Vernon was there staying at a place called "Mickys Bar", Elvis would go there every evening and stay there the whole evening talking to his daddy and playing a piano they had there, that is how close they were, every minute they could be together they were.

When Vernon's health deteriorated in the 70s he had a heart attack Elvis was beside himself, worried sick he might lose his rock, his Daddy. While Vernon was in hospital, he met a nurse he fell in love with, Sandy Miller, Dee moved out of his house in Dolan Drive, this then allowed Elvis to have a bedroom in the house which he went to often to get some peace and would talk to his daddy all day there.

When Vernon was well enough Elvis could not wait to introduce him on stage again, the love between them was evident for everyone to see. When Elvis died, I believe Vernon died of a broken heart, he just could not go on without his boy. I have been told he would lay a red rose on Elvis's grave every day and would spend most of the day in Elvis's bedroom crying for his son. Except for the time he spent investigating his son's death, which Vernon was convinced was murder, it is said not only did Vernon prove his son was murdered by someone close to Elvis, but he found out who.

Elvis and his Daddy tinkering with a motor bike like any other father and son.

LISA

Elvis's greatest achievement he said was having Lisa-Marie his daughter, he loved her above everything. In her early life it was Elvis and her nanny who looked after his little Buttonhead. Cilla was hardly ever there, when the family photos were taken Lisa cried when the photographer tried to put Lisa on Cillas lap, she literally did not know who she was, after the divorce in which Elvis regretfully agreed they should have equal custody, Elvis pinned for Lisa all the time when she was not with him, and he never missed a birthday or Christmas with her even if he was on tour, he was always there for her when he was needed, like when she had her tonsils out, for Elvis, Lisa always came first. If Lisa wanted snow they would get in the jet and find snow, for Lisa this was not unusual because this was her daddy who always did things on the spare of the moment and loved doing it for Lisa, for the joy it gave her gave him the most joy. Lisa brought sunshine into a life later filled with sorrow for Elvis, he knew she loved him because he was her daddy and no other reason, and he was a really fun daddy.

Of course Lisa knew exactly who her daddy was and one of Elvis's proudest moments was when she said for the first time that her daddy was 'Alvis Presley king of rock and roll', she eventually got to pronounce his name correctly, but would tease Elvis by calling him Alvis, and he would tell her 'no to you my name is Daddy', and Lisa also enjoyed telling the fans at the gate who her daddy was too.

Elvis is reported to have said, "I guess my favourite one (memory) now is when Lisa was born when I first held her, you know? She was so-so tiny-precious and beautiful. I know all babies look beautiful to their parent, but she was special. I guess because I realized she was my child - mine to care for and it was a special feeling. "You know, if you look into your child's eyes and they look back at you, you can easily see what trust really is - and it's scary, because they have such perfect love, without question they have faith. A pity - is that so many parents don't take the time anymore, to really look into their child's eyes." As a child life was hard for Elvis and he was determined his daughter would never endure what he had. Elvis could never bring himself to chastise Lisa because he knew how that felt, the few times he had tried to even tell her off, it was Elvis who got upset, not Lisa, he worshiped his daughter. Cilla has said that Elvis was frightened to carry Lisa as a baby down the stairs, in case he might drop her.

For Lisa after the divorce, it was confusing for her, her daddy was fun and loving and lavished her with anything she wanted, then she had to leave the wonder-world of her daddies and go to Cilla who was cold and did not like Elvis lavishing gifts on her. Cilla has admitted she never actually wanted Lisa and was jealous of her. Cilla was always consumed with her latest boyfriend and Lisa felt alone when she was with Cilla, she would stay in her bedroom listening to records. Elvis was acutely aware that his daughter was only happy when she was with him and had planned to get sole custody of Lisa when he died, Lisa was also, the reason he was going to give up touring and make movies again, so he could spend all his time with Lisa.

After Elvis died, Lisa's life changed forever. Straight after he died instead of comforting her daughter Cilla took her latest boyfriend to Europe and put a grieving Lisa aged 9 into summer camp, this alone should show you how cold and heartless Cilla was to her daughter, Cilla also would not allow photos of Elvis in her house in case they upset whoever she was going out with at the time. Mike Edwards tells in his book, who lived with Cilla for some time, that Lisa's only friends were the cook and her husband, and she would sit with them talking about her daddy. When Cilla found out she fired them, Lisa was alone again. Mike felt sorry for Lisa, Cilla was always pursuing her career and leaving Lisa with Mike who told Cilla he lusted after Lisa. Mike sexually molested Lisa for three years and Cilla knew, if Mike could not look after Lisa, then Cilla would leave Lisa with her parents which Mike said Lisa did not like at all. Mike also tells of Cilla beating up poor Lisa in the back of a car and making so much noise a neighbour phoned the police.

 Cilla led Lisa a dog's life, even stealing from her. For all her woes growing up with a cold mother who was totally indifferent to her Lisa has turned out remarkably well and I am sure this is all because she knew what real love was with her daddy who adored her more than anything. The memory of her daddy is something she would never forget, Lisa once said in an interview that she always felt safe loved and protected when she was with her daddy, something she has never felt since. She said Graceland was the place she felt so much love and happiness with Elvis, was always her home and said it will never be sold.

 Out of all the family photos taken that day this is the one Elvis had in his wallet, just him and Lisa, no Cilla.

CHARLIE

Elvis said to Charlie "that every king needed a court jester and Charlie was his", but Charlie was much more than that, I think out of all of them Charlie loved Elvis the most and I think like Larry they were destined to be friends, both had met Elvis years before they had actually become friends. Charlie was the singer with the Foggy River Boys, he used to stand on a crate because he was so small, Charlie and his group and Elvis were both on the Red Foley show in Memphis in 1956 when they met briefly, Elvis thought Charlie standing on the box was funny. They didn't meet again till they were stationed at fort hood and then on the voyage over to Europe I have read Charlie kept Elvis sane on the voyage and kept his spirits up, you must remember it was a really dark time for Elvis as he had just lost his mother, once in Germany Charlie found out where Elvis was, it wasn't difficult as the papers were full of it and Charlie became Elvis's lifelong friend.

Most people think of Charlie as the guy who got the water and scarves, put the cape on and sang back-up, but most people have no idea how nervous Elvis was about going on stage and some have said without Charlie there to back him up Elvis might not have got back on stage, that is how much Elvis relied on Charlie, in some ways it was like there was a special connection or code between them, whatever

Elvis was about to do on stage Charlie was intuitively ready for it, like throwing his guitar to Charlie.

When most of the other MMs moved out of Graceland and /or went to L.A. Charlie stayed with Elvis, he was always there for Elvis and Charlie kept true to Elvis's ethos, he never bad mouthed any of the people in Elvis's life in public as some did and he had lots of stories to tell so I have been told. Charlie always defended Elvis unlike so many of the rest. Charlie never got married until years after Elvis died, he was so committed to Elvis. In Charlies  book he tells a story of how one day he said to Elvis to get into the car and when Elvis asked why to begin with Charlie wouldn't tell him, but after they had driven a bit Charlie told Elvis he was taking him to hospital cause that was where he needed to be, how sad none of the others ever did that for Elvis, only Charlie looked out for Elvis like that. Many have claimed to have been Elvis's best friend, but I think only Charlie was.

LARRY GELLAR

I think like Charlie Hodge, Larry was destined to become friends with Elvis, both had chance meetings with Elvis before they got to know him. Larry met Elvis after a concert in L.A. when he was about 16years old, eight years before he became Elvis's hairdresser, from the first day he worked for Elvis it was clear they would be good friends and Larry became much more than Elvis's hairdresser. In Larry Elvis sensed someone he could be open with about his search for the truth of the universe and spirituality. Elvis had found that he had to be guarded with what he told most people they did not understand his search for knowledge and often mocked him for it, but Larry did not because Larry was also a seeker. Unfortunately many of those around Elvis did not appreciate his new friend they wanted Elvis to be a country hick only interested in beer, football and girls, which of course Elvis never was but some of them were and that's how they preferred Elvis to be, even though Elvis tried his hardest to make them see beyond their own upbringing to see outside the box and all the possibilities the universe held they would not, and so it drew Elvis and Larry closer together and the others grew jealous of their friendship, they reverted to their own closed boxes and called Larry names as they have no real way to compete.

Sadly, it was not only some of Elvis's other friends who were jealous of the time Elvis spent with him discussing all sorts of things like reincarnation, numerology, psychic abilities, healing, and many other things that Elvis dedicated himself to in his quest, as with everything Elvis did, he put every moment he could into trying to understand the universe and the forces within it.

Elvis's then-girlfriend Priscilla was also jealous of Larry and the time Elvis spent with him and jealous of the fact that Elvis tried to teach others what he had found, Elvis tried to include her but she did not or would not understand, Elvis spent more and more time in his pursuit of knowledge and spent more time meditating and going to the 'Self-Realization Fellowship Lake Shrine' in Pacific Palisades studying eastern philosophy, one of Elvis's books was 'Autobiography of a Yogi', so taken and inspire by this place and what he learned there Elvis decided he wanted to give everything up and become a monk, for Elvis where better could he continue his learning. Priscilla and Elvis's manager Parker laid all of this squarely on Larry and blamed him for the transformation Elvis had taken.

I think personally even without Larry Elvis would have found his way there as I am sure on a spiritual level it called to him, there he found solace and peace. Sadly, for Elvis, Priscilla and

Parker were not about to let that happen, Priscilla made Elvis burn all his spiritual books.

Parker while he had invited Larry and his family to his house had his own heavy's turn Larry's house upside down, Larry got the message and frightened for his family decided with a heavy heart that he must distance himself from Elvis, but as fate would have it several years later, they met again in Vegas and their friendship rekindled although Elvis had never given up on Larry and had watched his career from afar, and now without Priscilla there and Parkers influence on Elvis at a low ebb their friendship and search for the truth of the universe continued for the rest of Elvis's life. Larry has written several books about Elvis all of which I would recommend, curiously Larry was also born on the 8th as Elvis was, and as was I.

CONFIDENCE

Some people think Elvis had a lot of confidence, but that is not true at all, he had bravado and he had learned to laugh at himself before others did, but he had no confidence in his own abilities and no self-worth. Elvis literally had to many times be pushed onto the stage, so low and fragile was his confidence, in fact JD said if it weren't for Charlie being on stage with him, they would have never got him on stage, of course he was talking about the late 60s and 70s, Elvis was terrified that his fans would abandon him, or boo him off the stage as they had done once in Vegas in the 50s, it was why he hated doing Vegas cause he knew most there were not his fans and they were just there for a show, not him, but once on stage and he heard the cheers he transformed into his image, but underneath he was still the timid, shy man, people thought of as humble.

Elvis was also terrified of flying because his mother installed it into him to be because she was, he even went to Hawaii by boat in the 50s, come the 70s he had to fly his schedule was so exhausting it would not allow anything else, but Elvis was still terrified of flying and would have panic attacks if there was bad turbulence, but as in the rest of his life it did not make him give up, no he decided to try to overcome his fear of flying by learning to fly his jet himself, not an easy thing to do by any means, but he did it. To me this shows his strength of character, his mother might have beat his ego and pride out of him and given him no sense of self-worth, but his underlying spirit was still there, we can only imagine what he might have accomplished had she been different with him.

He told Kathy Westmoreland no one would remember him after he had been dead for two years, because he had never done anything of note or worth to be remembered for, so unconfident was he in his own abilities, his confidence that his mother knocked out of him at a young age never grew, how could he trust those around him when he knew they would say anything to get more out of him. Had it not been for his mother he would have been confident and had pride in his achievements and an ego to match, but he had none. One time in the 50s when he was playing near home he invited his mother to a concert of his, after the show he is all excited, his passion showing, and in front of all of his friends and fans who had gathered backstage she told him how disgusted she was with him and what an embarrassment he was to her not being able to control himself, can you imagine how mortified he was, he never invited her to watch him again.

So desperate was he for people to like him he allowed himself to be used and pushed around by them, frightened of confrontation, and they knew it so they took him for all he was worth, eventually most left except Charlie he was the only one true friend Elvis had, when the Wests and Hebler had to be fired Vernon had to do it cause it was beyond Elvis to do it, he could not be 'nasty' to someone even if they deserved it. What other man would let a woman boss him around like Cilla or Linda or Ginger did, Cilla made him burn his books to keep her from nagging at him and wear his hair how she wanted, Linda made him disinfect his mouth, no wonder she was hardly ever on tour or at Vegas with him, no matter what she says the photos prove different, he didn't have it in him to show her the door like most would, he just capitulated and did as he was told like a naughty little boy would, instead to try to get her out of Graceland he bought her a house and paid for an apartment in Los Angeles for her, but still she would not go, as she said in her an interview the perks were too good. The truest thing Red ever said was Elvis was a boy trapped in a man's body and he was, never was he allowed to make decisions himself. Control of his life went from his mother to Parker to Cilla and the rest. By the 70s Elvis had realised what his mother had done to him was wrong, and he started to talk about it, he talks about it in an interview, and he told his girlfriends, some took advantage of insecurities.

On his TCB oath the first words are 'More self-respect' Elvis

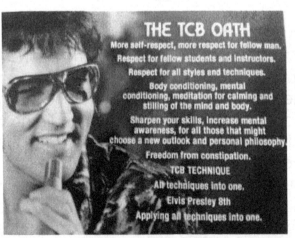

knew he had none and virtually no one had any for him and 'freedom from constipation', which had dogged him all his life. So, no Elvis did not have confidence, but he was a great acto

THE 70s

A lot of people still seem to have no idea how tough it was for Elvis to be Elvis especially in the 70s. It would seem most of the people who knew Elvis in the 70s had no empathy or sympathy for everything Elvis was going through in the seventies, most men when they turn 40 have a midlife crisis, some buy a flash car or get a young girlfriend or change their job but not one of them are under the huge amount of stress Elvis was.

Elvis had a lot to be depressed about in the 70s especially, anyone else would have crumbled under the pressure, the fact he did not shows how strong he was. His wife, soon to be ex was parading her lover around Vegas trying to upset him and undermine him. In 75 the papers were full of pictures saying he was fat and forty and couldn't do it anymore. Elvis was terrified of losing Lisa, especially after Cilla ran off with her with Mike Stone and he did not know where she was for more than two weeks. Elvis also got constant death threats; he knew the mob wanted him dead because he had undercover FBI men in his band in Vegas so they could spy on them, remember Elvis was also D.E.A.

His father had heart attacks and Elvis was frightened his father was going to die. Linda was running around with his keyboard player and threatening Elvis, so he could not make her leave Graceland, he bought her a house to keep her quiet, so yes, he had a lot to be depressed about.

For most men just hitting 40 makes them depressed and they do not got the whole world watching, telling them they are over the hill, his health wasn't great with his colon problem and glaucoma which was putting him in danger of losing his eyesight, he had viral arthritis which made every bone in his body ache and acute constipation, who wouldn't be depressed. Every time he went on stage, he risked his eyesight because of the bright lights and flashes, but he kept on because he loved his fans, if anything people should be saying HOW COURAGEOUS Elvis was that he did not crumble. When he finally got rid of Linda, he tried to start a new life with Ginger, which sadly failed.

Elvis also lost several people he knew that died in the 70s including a girlfriend, Mary Kathleen Selph in June 72 who was on her way to Graceland late one night when she had a car accident, Elvis blamed himself because she was on her way to see him, he was inconsolable. His favourite cousin Bobbie Jane Ayers Wrenn killed herself New Year's Eve 76, they waited till after Elvis had finished his concert to tell him, he immediately cancelled the New Years Eve party and went straight back to Memphis, again he was inconsolable, but he never gave up, he was determined to start a new career and get Lisa back.

Elvis had a physical every year for his insurance with Lloyds of London, he talks about the one he had in 76 in the Red West phone call, and he had passed the one in 77.

These pseudo autopsy programs on TV do not have access to Elvis's medical records or autopsy any more than we do, all they do is sensationalise to get people to watch, they do not care about the truth, only ratings, I have heard some stupid things said on those programs, like Elvis's intestines were twice as long as they should have been, firstly it is impossible and secondly we know Elvis had barium meal in his intestines at time of death, the only reason for that is because he had had an x-ray, within the last two weeks before he died of his intestines quite possibly as part of the physical for Lloyds, and if there had been any problem with his intestines they would have seen it and done something about it, but there was not, even Dr Francisco in a Memphis newspaper said that "Elvis did not have an impacted colon at the time of his death."

The other one that is often quoted and is also rubbish is Elvis's heart was twice the size it should have been, don't forget Elvis was an athlete so just as with all athletes his heart would have been bigger than an average heart, it is a muscle and muscles that work out get bigger, just like his lungs were bigger than average because he was a singer, when Elvis had his physical they had him running on a treadmill while wired up to an ECG machine had there been anything wrong with his heart it would have showed up then so please do not believe these programs use your common-sense and think about it, if you have any knowledge of anatomy you know I am right.

Yes, Elvis did have problems he took medication for, but don't forget he was out riding his Harley two days before his death, a heavy bike that you need to be fit to manoeuvre, and the night before he died, we are told he was playing racquetball if he had heart problem he could not have.
Elvis had medication for: -
Viral Arthritis, back then it was called Reiter's syndrome and being double-jointed/hypermobile it exacerbated it and was possibly the cause of his other ailment like Migraines, Glaucoma and Insomnia, although he had suffered with insomnia for most of his life as well, but Reiter's would have exacerbated it, in Dr Nicks book he said he once withdrew Elvis's sleep meds thinking he would eventually fall asleep naturally, but after about 4 days and nights without sleep Dr Nick knew it was not something Elvis just took on a whim like some would have you believe but that he needed sleep meds.
Elvis was also a sleepwalker and had been since childhood, especially when stressed, which he was constantly in the 70s, and most times he slept he had nightmares, adding to the stress and depression.

He had also suffered from constipation all his life which occasionally resulted in his colon twisting due to lazy bowel, (Lisa has also inherited a lazy bowel too, it was not something that just happened in the 70s).

Diabetes, which Elias Ghanem gave Elvis with his sleep diet.

Hypertension. (Who wouldn't be with all the stress Elvis was under).

So PLEASE DO NOT BELIEVE these pseudo-scientific programs, they are all bogus. In case you are wondering I have a diploma in anatomy and physiology, so I do know a bit about how the body works. Elvis's last concert, his legs as strong as ever they were to be able to squat down like this.

NOT JUST A SINGER

Elvis became a star because of his exceptional voice and style, but Elvis did not want to make it as a singer, he wanted to be a movie star, as a teenager he got a job as an usherette at a local cinema so he could study all the great actors, and that is what he wanted to be, a great actor, and Elvis fashioned his looks after Tony Curtis, who was at the time a box office smash who all the girls liked. When he first made it big as a singer, he thought his dream of becoming a great actor would be realised as he got the chance to star in some good movies, and he thought his dream was going to come true.

As we all know Parker, who never had any faith in Elvis's abilities as an actor or singer had ideas of his own. Instead of letting Elvis know he might be excused from the draft, being an only son, the bread-winner for not only his immediate family but all his extended family, and especially because his mother being critically ill, Parker had his own ideas and instead of putting both Elvis's health and well-being and that of his mother he just persuaded the draft board to give Elvis an extension so he could finish the movie Elvis was doing, this put even more strain on Gladys knowing her son would soon be removed from her and while Elvis was still in basic training she died, some say he never recovered from her death or forgave himself.

Parkers mission was simple to make as much money out of Elvis and his fans as he possibly could and fresh out of the army the once rebel was now the all-American wholesome homecoming boy, Elvis was even offered a part in ''West Side Story'' in 1961, but Parker said no, the rebel image of before the army was gone. Parker made so much of the fact Elvis had been in the army that several movies were based on the fact and Parker's money-making machine was born, never the matter what it did to Elvis physically or emotionally or to his image which was carefully staged at every turn, making an image that had little at all to do with who Elvis really was or what he wanted to be.

By now Elvis was not some raw kid, he had seen more of the world and what was going on in it, and he had a new purpose in life, he wanted to help anyone and everyone and the world in general as much as he could. Elvis had always had a thirst for knowledge and whereas in his pre-army days he delighted in reading medical journals now he read everything he could so he could learn as much as he could about the world. He was fascinated by the ancients, from the Mayans to the Egyptians and every other ancient culture he could read about and by all the world's religions. In the mid to late 60s he wanted to become a Buddhist monk and for those who do not know, they do not believe in a god, but Elvis found their teachings extremely peaceful and just what he needed, he would often go to the Self-Realization Fellowship in Los Angeles, but alas once again his dream was thwarted this time not only by Parker but Parker's ally Cilla. This did not stop Elvis even when she made him burn all his books, and Parker threatened and chased away his only friend who understood his quest for knowledge

Larry Geller. Within two years Cilla was gone to 'find herself' and once again his quest continued, and he started on another project that concerned itself with helping people, The Tribe of Dan, but once again Cilla who still wielded a great influence over Elvis because of Lisa stopped him doing it, but this never changed his mind on who he really to be and what he really wanted to do, which was to bring east and west together in mutual harmony and understanding, a vast task by anyone's standards.

Elvis though was not just anyone, and he had a great influence over many people not just other singers and movie stars and boxers but world leaders everyone who was anyone and everyone else wanted to meet the king, and many leaders, Kings, Queen, Princes, and Princess had already met him. By the seventies Elvis had a vast knowledge of just about everything that had happened in history on the planet, ancient and new and all religions, he didn't stop there he was interested in all things paranormal, in science fiction and science fact, his repertoire of books was vast, from Chariots of the Gods, to the book of Toa, as well as books on reading auras, colour therapy, you name it he had read about it. He believed in reincarnation, in fact he believed he had been Jesus in a previous incarnation, he was telepathic, telekinetic, he could astral travel, he believed in the Akashic record, and he was a healer as well as being psychic, he also believed in alternative healing techniques like acupuncture. He also believed in prophecy too, and virtually every night of his life he dreamt he would be murdered. Contrary to the image so carefully crafted by Parker and others, Elvis was not a sex-crazed violent druggy. In fact he was just opposite, he did not believe in one-night stands at all, for him there was no such thing as casual sex, for him there was only making love, which meant with someone you loved, and many women who knew him have attested to this, he liked female company, he liked to talk and read and sing to them but that was it. He hated being alone, especially sleeping alone because of the nightmares and because from childhood he had sleepwalked, so he needed someone to watch him, once when he had slept alone, one of the MMs went to check on him they found him sleep walking on the fire escape ladder.

Most people are not aware that from 1969 onwards Elvis was offered at least four movies that I know of that could have changed his life and career and opened him up to the wider general public, he was offered a part in John Waynes "True Grit" movie, of course Parker turned it down because he would not allow Elvis to share top billing with anyone, and as always Parker wanted complete control and a huge sum of money, Elvis was also offered the part that eventually went to Meatloaf in the "Rocky Horror Show", Elvis was also offered the part of Valentino in the story of his life, no doubt because Elvis looked so good in "Harem Scarum", and then there is the one most people know about which was "A Star is Born", Elvis was so excited to be asked to star in this, asked personally by Barbra Streisand herself, Red said Elvis phone him the night she asked him, Elvis was over the moon about it and really enthusiastic about it, but once again Parker because he would not have control turned it down, Elvis was devastated, any one of these would have launched his career as a serious actor, and as so many times in the past Parker would not allow Elvis to do what he really wanted to do.

By the mid-70s he knew what he must do, he wanted to quit touring and go back to making good movies, this would also give him more time for what he wanted to do. He had already fired several people and there was a long list of who else was to go, including Parker. Elvis had a lot of plans for him and his daughter Lisa. In the March of 77, he had his will rewritten not just to remove Cilla which was a large part of it, but to remove all the other hangers-on from his will as well, now this bit is important and it shows Elvis had no thought of dying any time soon, he left his estate to ' HIS CHILDREN' meaning that he thought he was going to live a good while longer and have more children. He had Charlie as one witness because he knew he could trust Charlie not to say anything to any of the others and he had Ginger as his other witness knowing she thought she was above talking to anyone; it also proves that by then he had no intention of marrying her as someone who is a witness cannot benefit from a will. (By April he had met Alicia Kerwin, who supposedly was waiting for Elvis in Portland at the concert that did not happen in August, and I know of two different women Elvis tried to get in contact with in the June but because of circumstances neither happened).

New Year's Eve 1976/77 President Jimmy Carter personally phoned Elvis and asked him to be his 'Special Advisor for Youth', of course Elvis said yes this was the chance he had been waiting for, his dreams and his reason for being were finally starting to happen, sadly it never happened because of that horrendous book the Wests and Hebler had published, not only did they destroy Elvis but the world's chance for peace. Just imagine eventually Elvis could have become a World Ambassador for Peace. Elvis unlike anybody else could have opened doors that would not have been opened for anyone else, this man was such a phenomenon that everyone in the world knew who he was, more people knew who Elvis was by his first name than knew who Jesus was. This is a man whose aura was so great you could 'feel' him coming before he entered the room. Elvis was the man everyone wanted to meet and who everyone said was the most charming man they had ever met, I know in my heart he could have got people and nations talking who then would not even look at each other, and do not forget this man knew about every culture and religion there had ever been, so he could have shown a real interest in other nations and their problems in a way no one else could have, had it not have been for that book and had he not been murdered, think what a better world we would have today. Elvis might have been a musical genius, but his real calling was not to be a singer but to bring the world together. Elvis is said to have told Kathy Westmoreland that within two years of his death no one would remember him because he had not done anything noteworthy, the fact is hardly anybody does remember the real Elvis, they remember the singer and entertainer, but not who he really was, which is why it annoys me so much when people say his music will live on or he will always be remembered for his singing, because that was NOT what Elvis wanted to be remembered for, Elvis wanted people to remember the real him, not Parkers manufactured phony image that bore so little resemblance to who Elvis really was.

Elvis was the most caring, considerate, compassionate, empathic, kind, spiritual, old soul the world has probably ever known, he was most definitely not just a singer.

FUTURE PLANS

On the 3rd of March 1977, Elvis started to put his plans he had been making since the previous summer into action. He had had his will rewritten, this marked the first big step for his future, not only was Cilla excluded from his will but so too were all the hangers-on and leeches. Elvis had finally come to the hard decision that they were not there for him, but what they could get out of him, and what being associated with him did for them. He made prevision for his grandmother Minnie-Mae (Dodger) and his Aunt Delta that they could live at Graceland as long as they wanted. Some people will tell you that this a will of dying man, they could not be more wrong, this was the will of a man who was starting to take charge of his life, admittedly a bit late in life, but the 70s had been hell for Elvis for many reasons and it made him take stock of everything and everyone around him, it had given him a new perspective on life and who and what was important. In his will it mentions all his children, although Lisa is mentioned by name as well, it seems to me that this is a man who thought he had many years of life left to live and that he would have more children in the future.

He had Charlie Hodge as one witness and Ginger Alden as the other, this tells me a couple of things. Charlie was the only one he truly trusted, Elvis knew Charlie was there because of love not money and he would stand by him,

Elvis had lost faith in most of the others, (I do not include Larry in the others as Larry always did his own thing and never lived with Elvis or off Elvis as the others had). It also tells me he had no intention by now of marrying Ginger either, because someone who witnesses a will cannot receive anything from it, he had her sign it because he knew she never talked to anyone he knew, so she would not be telling anyone either. Elvis was a lot shrewder than most think.

After the will had been signed, they departed for Elvis's last holiday in Hawaii. Elvis loved Hawaii and this time apart from a relaxing holiday there were two other reasons for going, as always Ginger demanded that some of her family accompanied them, what she did not realise was it was make or break as far as their relationship was concerned. Elvis had hoped that Ginger would spend all her time with him and make him feel that he was the most important thing to her, but even this holiday was not enough to make her show him the love he needed from her and most of the time she spent with her family sightseeing, shopping and on the beach, all on Elvis's dime of course. The money he could care less about, but he knew when he was being took and she was doing it in grand style, so most of the time he spent alone in his room and not with her. Elvis did however take a look around the island according to Larry with him for a place to either buy or rent for when he put the final parts of his plans into action.

At the end of the August concert tour Elvis had planned to fire Parker, his manager, and many others including Joe Esposito, who was suing Elvis, Elvis was going to 'clean house' and 'cut out all the deadwood' and those who were not there for him. Someone overheard Elvis discuss his plans with Larry and reported back to Parker because in the April Parker tried to sell his contract as manager with Elvis but could not get the money he wanted. This settled Elvis's fate and in the August before the tour started, they murdered him.

Had Elvis lived he had planned to get full custody of Lisa, go to Hawaii for an extended time to get as healthy as possible and start making good movies, even direct, which he had always wanted to do, he had had plenty of offers in the 70s, but Parker had knocked each one back, being frightened he might lose control of his cash cow, he always insisted on having the final say and after Elvis did what he wanted in the 68 Special Parker made sure Elvis was kept on a tight lead. It is said Elvis already had a new manager lined up, Tom Hulet has been mentioned as a possible person. Elvis might have even been able to salvage the offer of being President Carters offer to be Special Advisor for Youth after the bad press for that insidious book had died down and Elvis had had the chance to prove they were liars, and he was not the person they tried to portray him as.

DID YOU KNOW

Most people know that Bruce Springsteen idolised Elvis, and that John Lennon famously said, "Before Elvis there was nothing", but did you know that Jimi Hendrix also idolised Elvis, he had seen Elvis when he was a boy in the late 50s and saw Elvis perform at an open-air concert, right there and then the young Jimi decided he was going to be like Elvis when he grew up, later when he came to London to promote his career and things were not going well he watched the Elvis movie 'Kid Galahad' for inspiration, and when Jimi played Woodstock he wore the same guitar strap as Elvis had worn in the 68 Special to pay homage to his idol.

Barry White a famous soul singer of the 70s was a jailbird when he was younger and while sitting in prison one day Elvis singing 'It's now or Never' came over the radio, right there and then he decided to give up his bad ways and become a famous singer. Just two stories of many of famous people whose lives were changed forever by Elvis.

Elvis never won an Oscar for any of his movies, he was however recognised by the indigenous Americans for his 'constructive portrayal of a man of Indian blood' in Flaming Star ~ 1960 " Elvis Presley was inducted into the Los Angeles Tribal Council by Chief Wha-Nee-Ota, and contrary to popular opinion Elvis did make some other good movies in amongst all he bad beach girlie movies he was contracted to make, that in his own words made him physically ill to make.

Elvis did not go unnoticed by those in the profession though, and as I said earlier, John Wayne wanted Elvis to play alongside of him in the movie 'True Grit', and others wanted Elvis to play Valentino in a biographical movie about him. Elvis was also sort after to play Eddie in the movie 'Rocky Horror Picture Show', the part eventually went to Meatloaf. Barbara Streisand went to Las Vegas to ask Elvis personally to play in the movie 'A Star is Born', that's how much she wanted Elvis to be in her movie, but sadly, Parker Elvis's manager turned all these movies that could have given Elvis a second chance to be an acting star he always wanted to be because Parker would not have complete control. Elvis never wanted to be a singing superstar, in the beginning, he really wanted to be a great actor, and why he got an after-school job in a theatre so he could study the actors on the big screen. These people would not have wanted Elvis in their movies had they not thought he was a good actor. The fact he always did his movies to his best abilities and made it look so easy with a smile on his face when he was dying inside because of some of the parts he had to play, no one would have guessed how much it troubled him to do these beach girlie movies, when he so desperately wanted to serious acting and to be taken seriously as an actor proves just what a good actor he was in a way.

Proof a lot of people had confidence in Elvis's acting abilities.

People

IN THE NEWS

From Our Wire Services

Elvis Offered Role

Elvis Presley

Rock singer Elvis Presley has been offered $2.5 million to portray silent screen star Rudolph Valentino in a stage and movie musical. Producer Bill Sargent said Wednesday he will bring the musical "Ciao Rudy," now playing Rome with Marcello Mastroianni in the lead, to the United States early next year. He plans a four-week engagement at Radio City Music Hall in New York, with one of the live performances filmed and released to theaters worldwide. Sargent said the $2.5 million offer would be the most money ever paid an entertainer for a combined four-week stage and movie performance. Presley gave no immediate reply.

ELVIS'S LAST WILL AND TESTAMENT

The Will of Elvis Presley
Last Will And Testament Of Elvis A. Presley,
Deceased Filed August 22, 1977
I, Elvis A. Presley, a resident and citizen of
Shelby County, Tennessee, being of sound mind
and disposing memory, do hereby make, publish
and declare this instrument to be my last will and
testament, hereby revoking any and all wills and
codicils by me at any time heretofore made.

Item I
Debts, Expenses and Taxes
I direct my Executor, hereinafter named, to pay
all of my matured debts and my funeral
expenses, as well as the costs and expenses of
the administration of my estate, as soon after my
death as practicable. I further direct that all
estate, inheritance, transfer and succession
taxes which are payable by reason under this
will, be paid out of my residuary estate; and I
hereby waive on behalf of my estate any right to
recover from any person any part of such taxes
so paid. My Executor, in his sole discretion, may
pay from my domiciliary estate all or any portion
of the costs of ancillary administration and
similar proceedings in other jurisdictions.

Item II
Instruction Concerning Personal Property:
Enjoyment in Specie. I anticipate that included

as a part of my property and estate at the time of my death will be tangible personal property of various kinds, characters, and values, including trophies and other items accumulated by me during my professional career. I hereby specifically instruct all concerned that my Executor, herein appointed, shall have complete freedom and discretion as to disposal of any and all such property so long as he shall act in good faith and in the best interest of my estate and my beneficiaries, and his discretion so exercised shall not be subject to question by anyone whomsoever.

I hereby expressly authorize my Executor and my Trustee, respectively and successively, to permit any beneficiary of any and all trusts created hereunder to enjoy in specie the use or benefit of any household goods, chattels, or other tangible personal property (exclusive of choses in action, cash, stocks, bonds or other securities) which either my Executor or my Trustees may receive in kind, and my Executor and my Trustees shall not be liable for any consumption, damage, injury to or loss of any tangible property so used, nor shall the beneficiaries of any trusts hereunder or their executors of administrators be liable for any consumption, damage, injury to or loss of any tangible personal property so used.

Item III
Real Estate
If I am the owner of any real estate at the time of my death, I instruct and empower my Executor and my Trustee (as the case may be) to hold such real estate for investment, or to sell same, or any portion thereof, as my Executor or my Trustee (as the case may be) shall in his sole judgment determines to be for the best interest of my estate and the beneficiaries thereof.

Item IV
Residuary Trust
After payment of all debts, expenses and taxes as directed under Item I hereof, I give, devise, and bequeath all the rest, residue, and remainder of my estate, including all lapsed legacies and devices, and any property over which I have a power of appointment, to my Trustee, hereinafter named, in trust for the following purposes:
(a) The Trustees is directed to take, hold, manage, invest and reinvent the corpus of the trust and to collect the income therefrom in accordance with the rights, powers, duties, authority and discretion hereinafter set forth. The Trustee is directed to pay all the expenses, taxes and costs incurred in the management of the trust estate out of the income thereof.
(b) After payment of all expenses, taxes and costs incurred in the management of the expenses, taxes and costs incurred in the management of the trust estate, the Trustee is

authorizes to accumulate the net income or to pay or apply so much of the net income and such portion of the principal at any time and from time to time to time for health, education, support, comfortable maintenance and welfare of:

(1) My daughter, Lisa Marie Presley, and any other lawful issue I might have,

(2) my grandmother, Minnie Mae Presley,

(3) my father, Vernon E. Presley, and

(4) such other relatives of mine living at the time of my death who in the absolute discretion of my Trustees are in need of emergency assistance for any of the above mentioned purposes and the Trustee is able to make such distribution without affecting the ability of the trust to meet the present needs of the first three numbered categories of beneficiaries herein mentioned or to meet the reasonably expected future needs of the first three classes of beneficiaries herein mentioned. Any decision of the Trustee as to whether or not distribution, to any of the persons described hereunder shall be final and conclusive and not subject to question by any legatee or beneficiary hereunder.

(c) Upon the death of my Father, Vernon E. Presley, the Trustee is instructed to make no further distributions to the fourth category of beneficiaries and such beneficiaries shall cease to have any interest whatsoever in this trust.

(d) Upon the death of both my said father and my said grandmother, the Trustee is directed to divide the Residuary Trust into separate and equal trusts, creating one such equal trust for each of my lawful children then surviving and one such equal trust for the living issue collectively, if any, of any deceased child of mine. The share, if any, for the issue of any such deceased child, shall immediately vest in such issue in equal shares but shall be subject to the provisions of Item V herein. Separate books and records shall be kept for each trust, but it shall not be necessary that a physical division of the assets be made as to each trust.

The Trustee may from time to time distribute the whole or any part of the net income or principal from each of the aforesaid trusts as the Trustee, in its uncontrolled discretion, considers necessary or desirable to provide for the comfortable support, education, maintenance, benefit and general welfare of each of my children. Such distributions may be made directly to such beneficiary or to the guardian of the person of such beneficiary and without responsibility on my Trustee to see to the application of nay such distributions and in making such distributions, the Trustee shall take into account all other sources of funds known by the Trustee to be available for each respective beneficiary for such purpose.

(e) As each of my respective children attains the age of twenty-five (25) years and provided that both my father and my grandmother are deceased, the trust created hereunder for such child care terminate, and all the remainder of the assets then contained in said trust shall be distributed to such child so attaining the age of twenty-five (25) years outright and free of further trust.

(f) If any of my children for whose benefit a trust has been created hereunder should die before attaining the age of twenty- five (25) years, then the trust created for such a child shall terminate on his death, and all remaining assets then contained in said trust shall be distributed outright and free of further trust and in equal shares to the surviving issue of such deceased child but subject to the provisions of Item V herein; but if there be no such surviving issue, then to the brothers and sisters of such deceased child in equal shares, the issue of any other deceased child being entitled collectively to their deceased parent's share. Nevertheless, if any distribution otherwise becomes payable outright and free of trust under the provisions of this paragraph (f) of the Item IV of my will to a beneficiary for whom the Trustee is then administering a trust for the benefit of such beneficiary under provisions of this last will and testament, such distribution shall not be paid outright to such beneficiary but shall be added to and become a part of the trust so being administered for such beneficiary by the Trustee.

Item V
Distribution to Minor Children
If any share of corpus of any trust established under this will become distributable outright and free of trust to any beneficiary before said beneficiary has attained the age of eighteen (18) years, then said share shall immediately vest in said beneficiary, but the Trustee shall retain possession of such share during the period in which such beneficiary is under the age of eighteen (18) years, and, in the meantime, shall use and expend so much of the income and principal for the care, support, and education of such beneficiary, and any income not so expended with respect to each share so retained all the power and discretion had with respect to such trust generally.

Item VI
Alternate Distributees
In the event that all of my descendants should be deceased at any time prior to the time for the termination of the trusts provided for herein, then in such event all of my estate and all the assets of every trust to be created hereunder (as the case may be) shall then distributed outright in equal shares to my heirs at law per stripes.

Item VII
Unenforceable Provisions
If any provisions of this will are unenforceable, the remaining provisions shall, nevertheless, be carried into effect.

Item VIII
Life Insurance
If my estate is the beneficiary of any life
insurance on my life at the time of my death, I
direct that the proceeds therefrom will be used
by my Executor in payment of the debts ,
expenses and taxes listed in Item I of this will, to
the extent deemed advisable by the Executor.
All such proceeds not so used are to be used by
my Executor for the purpose of satisfying the
devises and bequests contained in Item IV
herein.

Item IX
Spendthrift Provision
I direct that the interest of any beneficiary in
principal or income of any trust created
hereunder shall not be subject to claims of
creditors or others, nor to legal process, and
may not be voluntarily or involuntarily alienated
or encumbered except as herein provided. Any
bequests contained herein for any female shall
be for her sole and separate use, free from the
debts, contracts and control of any husband she
may ever have.

Item X
Proceeds From Personal Services
All sums paid after my death (either to my estate
or to any of the trusts created hereunder) and
resulting from personal services rendered by me
during my lifetime, including, but not limited to,
royalties of all nature, concerts, motion picture

contracts, and personal appearances shall be considered to be income, notwithstanding the provisions of estate and trust law to the contrary.

Item XI
Executor and Trustee
I appoint as executor of this, my last will and testament, and as Trustee of every trust required to be created hereunder, my said father.

I hereby direct that my said father shall be entitled by his last will and testament, duly probated, to appoint a successor Executor of my estate, as well as a successor Trustee or successor Trustees of all the trusts to be created under my last will and testament.

If, for any reason, my said father be unable to serve or to continue to serve as Executor and/or as Trustee, or if he be deceased and shall not have appointed a successor Executor or Trustee, by virtue of his last will and testament as stated -above, then I appoint National Bank of Commerce, Memphis, Tennessee, or its successor or the institution with which it may merge, as successor Executor and/or as successor Trustee of all trusts required to be established hereunder.

None of the appointees named hereunder, including any appointment made by virtue of the last will and testament of my said father, shall be required to furnish any bond or security for performance of the respective fiduciary duties required hereunder, notwithstanding any rule of law to the contrary.

Item XII
Powers, Duties, Privileges and Immunities of the Trustee
Except as otherwise stated expressly to the contrary herein, I give and grant to the said Trustee (and to the duly appointed successor Trustee when acting as such) the power to do everything he deems advisable with respect to the administration of each trust required to be established under this, my last will and Testament, even though such powers would not be authorized or appropriate for the Trustee under statutory or other rules of law. By way of illustration and not in limitation of the generality of the foregoing grant of power and authority of the Trustee, I give and grant to him plenary power as follows:

(a)To exercise all those powers authorized to fiduciaries under the provisions of the Tennessee Code Annotated, Sections 35-616 to 35-618, inclusive, including any amendments thereto in effect at the time of my death, and the same are expressly referred to and incorporated herein by reference.

(b) Plenary power is granted to the Trustee, not only to relieve him from seeking judicial instruction, but to the extent that the Trustee deems it to be prudent, to encourage determinations freely to be made in favor of persons who are the current income beneficiaries. In such instances the rights of all subsequent beneficiaries are subordinate, and the Trustee shall not be answerable to any subsequent beneficiary for anything done or omitted in favor of a current income beneficiary may compel any such favorable or preferential treatment. Without in anywise minimizing or impairing the scope of this declaration of intent, it includes investment policy, exercise of discretionary power to pay or apply principal and income, and determination principal and income questions.

(c) It shall be lawful for the Trustee to apply any sum that is payable to or for the benefit of a minor (or any other person who in the Judgment of the Trustee, is incapable of making proper disposition thereof) by payments in discharge of the costs and expenses of educating, maintaining and supporting said beneficiary, or to make payment to anyone with whom said beneficiary resides or who has the care or custody of the beneficiary, temporarily or permanently, all without intervention of any guardian or like fiduciary. The receipt of anyone to whom payment is so authorized to be made shall be a complete discharge of the Trustees without obligation on his part to see to the further application hereto, and without regard to other resource that the beneficiary may have, or the duty of any other person to support the beneficiary.

(d) In Dealing with the Trustee, no grantee, pledge, vendee, mortgage, lessee or other transference of the trust properties, or any part thereof, shall be bound to inquire with respect to the purpose or necessity of any such disposition or to see to the application of any consideration therefore paid to the Trustee.

Item XIII
Concerning the Trustee and the Executor
(a)If at any time the Trustee shall have reasonable doubt as to his power, authority or duty in the administration of any trust herein created, it shall be lawful for the Trustee to obtain the advice and counsel of reputable legal counsel without resorting to the courts for instructions; and the Trustee shall be fully absolved from all liability and damage or detriment to the various trust estates of any beneficiary thereunder by reason of anything done, suffered or omitted pursuant to advice of said counsel given and obtained in good faith, provided that nothing contained herein shall be construed to prohibit or prevent the Trustee in all proper cases from applying to a court of competent jurisdiction for instructions in the administration of the trust assets in lieu of obtaining advice of counsel.

(b) In managing, investing, and controlling the various trust estates, the Trustee shall exercise the judgment and care under the circumstances then prevailing, which men of prudence discretion and judgment exercise in the management of their own affairs, not in regard to speculation, but in regard to the permanent disposition of their funds, considering the probable income as well as the probable safety of their capital, and, in addition, the purchasing power of income distribution to beneficiaries.

(c) My Trustee (as well as my Executor) shall be entitled to reasonable and adequate and adequate compensation for the fiduciary services rendered by him.

(d) My Executor and his successor Executor and his successor Executor shall have the same rights, privileges, powers and immunities herein granted to my Trustee wherever appropriate.

(e) In referring to any fiduciary hereunder, for purposes of construction, masculine pronouns may include a corporate fiduciary and neutral pronouns may include an individual fiduciary.

Item XIV
Law Against Perpetuities

(a) Having in mind the rule against perpetuities, I direct that (notwithstanding anything contained to the contrary in this last will and testament) each trust created under this will (except such trust created under this will (except such trusts as have heretofore vested in compliance with such rule or law) shall end, unless sooner terminated under other provisions of this will, twenty-one (21) years after the death of the last survivor of such of the beneficiaries hereunder as are living at the time of my death; and thereupon that the property held in trust shall be distributed free of all trust to the persons then entitled to receive the income and/or principal therefrom, in the proportion in proportion in which they are then entitled to receive such income.

(b) Notwithstanding anything else contained in this will to the contrary, I direct that if any distribution under this will become payable to a person for whom the Trustee is then administering a trust created hereunder for the benefit of such person, such distribution shall be made to such trust and not to the beneficiary outright, and the funds so passing to such trust shall become a part thereof as corpus and be administered and distributed to the same extent and purpose as if such funds had been a part of such a trust at its inception.

Item XV
Payment of Estate and Inheritance Taxes
Notwithstanding the provisions of Item X herein, I authorize my Executor to use such sums received by my estate after my death and resulting from my personal services as identified in Item X as he deems necessary and advisable in order to pay the taxes referred to in Item I of my said will.

In WITNESS WHEREOF, I, the said ELVIS A. PRESLEY, do hereunto set my hand and seal in the presence of two (2) competent witnesses, and in their presence do publish and declare this instrument to be my Last Will and Testament, this 3 day of March 1977.

[Signed by Elvis A. Presley]

ELVIS A. PRESLEY

The foregoing instrument, consisting of this and eleven (11) preceding typewritten pages, was signed, sealed, published and declared by ELVIS A. PRESLEY, the Testator, to be his Last Will and Testament, in our presence, and we, at his request and in his presence and in the presence of each other, have hereunto subscribed our names as witnesses, this 3 day of March 1977, at Memphis, Tennessee.

[Signed by Ginger Alden]

Ginger Alden residing at 4152 Royal Crest Place

[Signed by Charles F. Hodge]

Charles F. Hodge residing at 3764 Elvis Presley Blvd.

[Signed by Ann Dewey Smith]

Ann Dewey Smith residing at 2237 Court Avenue.

State of Tennessee County of Shelby

Ginger Alden, Charles F. Hodge, and Ann Dewey Smith, after being first duly sworn, make oath or affirm that the foregoing Last Will and Testament, in the sight and presence of us, the undersigned, who at his request and in his sight and presence, and in the sight and presence of each other, have subscribed our names as attesting witnesses on the 3 day of March, 1977, and we further make oath or affirm that the Testator was of sound mind and disposing memory and not acting under fraud, menace or undue influence of any person, and was more than eighteen (18) years of age; and that each of the attesting witnesses is more than eighteen (18) years of age.

[Signed by Ginger Alden]
Ginger Alden
[Signed by Charles F. Hodge]
Charles F. Hodge
[Signed by Ann Dewey Smith]
Ann Dewey Smith
Sworn To And Subscribed before me this 3 day of March, 1977.
Drayton Beecker Smith II Notary Public
My commission expires:
August 8, 1979
Admitted to probate and Ordered Recorded
August 22, 1977
Joseph W. Evans, Judge Recorded August 22, 1977
B.J. Dunavant, Clerk by: Jan Scott, D.C.

instrument to be my Last Will and Testament, this __3__ day

of __MARCH__ , ~~1976~~ 1977.

Elvis A. Presley
ELVIS A. PRESLEY

The foregoing instrument, consisting of this and eleven
(11) preceding typewritten pages, was signed, sealed, published
and declared by ELVIS A. PRESLEY, the Testator, to be his Last
Will and Testament, in our presence, and we, at his request and
in his presence and in the presence of each other, have hereunto
subscribed our names as witnesses, this __3__ day of __MARCH__
~~1976~~ 1977, at Memphis, Tennessee.

Ginger Alden residing at __4152 Royal Crest Plac__

Charles F. Hodge residing at __3764 Clarkshelp Blvd__
Ann Dewey Smith __2237 Court Avenue__

STATE OF TENNESSEE)
COUNTY OF SHELBY)

__GINGER ALDEN, CHARLES F. HODGE__ and __ANN DEWEY SMITH__,
after being first duly sworn, make oath or affirm that the foregoing Last Will and Testament was signed by ELVIS A. PRESLEY and
for and at that time acknowledged, published and declared by him
to be his Last Will and Testament, in the sight and presence of
us, the undersigned, who at his request and in his sight and
presence, and in the sight and presence of each other, have
subscribed our names as attesting witnesses on the __3__ day of
__MARCH__ , ~~1976~~ 1977, and we further make oath or affirm
that the Testator was of sound mind and disposing memory and
not acting under fraud, menace or undue influence of any person,

note Elvis's, Charlie's, and Ginger's signatures.

HOW I REMEMBER ELVIS TO BE

Elvis loved all kinds of animals, they gave him the sort of unconditional love he yearned for in a partner, there are many photos of him on his horses, but Sun was his favourite, and over the years he had quite a few dogs and other animals, he even could often be heard talking to the squirrels that ran free at Graceland.

Elvis's nails were always immaculately manicured even though he had the habit of biting his nails when he was really nervous and he was invariably nervous about something most of the time, and he had several ways to try and combat the habit, like using a cigar or cigarette as more of a prop than to actually smoke them, he even tried a pipe, and chewing gum, and putting his hands in his pockets anything to stop him biting his nails. So, Elvis loathed dirty fingernails on other people, he felt everyone should always try to look their best as he did. He liked his ladies to have elegant hands and feet too, with long legs and he liked his ladies to be just that, to act like ladies, he did not like them swearing or cussing as he would say. Elvis always liked his women to be well turned out and wearing something appropriate for the activity as he did. Elvis was very conscious of how he looked, never would he have stubble, he would be horrified at all the photos of him that have been changed to look as if he has, he was always clean shaven, he even carried around an electric shaver to make sure. He also liked his women in skirts or dresses, not trousers, after all, he was the man, he also found hairy macho women to upset his sensibilities.

He had this thing he would do where he would run his tongue under the top lip of his amore, and something he called the Chinese way, he also liked to rub noses too. Elvis was a very passionate, sensual, romantic, tender, and tactile man who liked the feel of soft things against his skin, like silk, he would often have the label in the neck of a shirt removed because it bothered him. Elvis loved beauty whether it was a statue of Apollo, a painting, or a beautiful woman, he soon found out to his cost that beauty on the outside did not mean beauty on the inside and he realised he needed a woman with an open mind who could keep up with him as he taught her all he knew, he liked to teach people things, to be their mentor. He would often ask about your dreams or even if he found a far-away look on your face he would want to know what you were thinking, and try and work out what it meant, even more so if you were trying to meditate with him, he wanted to know everything you saw, his thirst for knowledge was so great he took every opportunity to increase his knowledge, and he was usually very serious about it too.

Elvis loved his fans and often would be found at the gates of whichever property he was in talking to them, he needed their love, to be one of them almost, he talked to them about them and how they felt, and how they felt about him and whatever his latest record or movie and everything else, but not so much about him, he wanted to know what made them tick, he enjoyed their company and the feeling of normality they gave him, which is why his reputation was so important to him, he knew how easily people could be swayed to not like him, how tenuous his place at the top was, sadly since his death this has become true, no longer do they want to know the fun-loving ever giving generous man he was, and he was all of those things and so much more, super-intelligent, dynamic, a heart so big it would swallow you up in a minute and you would be grateful it did for the unconditional love he gave you. He had the capacity to be deadly serious one minute and the next rolling around on the floor laughing about something, he never hid his emotions unless it was because he knew it might hurt another, he did that a lot, hide himself, his real self so few really knew because he was frightened of upsetting them. He nearly always put others first unless doing so hurt someone else he cared for more. He was never conceited or arrogant although one could say as far as his music business was concerned, he had every right to be, because he was also frightened it

[116]

could all be taken from him in a flash. He never took it for granted.

Elvis never liked to throw anything away, some might say he was a hoarder, but it wasn't that, he did give things away, he gave lots of the things that had given to him away to those less fortunate than he was, being fortunate in some areas of his life was something he never forgot, so if someone gave him something it meant something to him, especially if they had made it just for him, put their love and time and effort into it, how could he give something like that away, these simple things his fans gave him meant so much more than lavish gifts some of his girlfriends and ex-wife bought him with his money. So, he gave his clothes to charity and other things like teddies to hospitals but throw them away no he could not do that.

Elvis did not like strong smells they upset his delicate sensibilities, unless of course it was something he liked the smell off like horses and roses, he liked roses, red ones. He was a very intricate person of many layers and contradictions but altogether it made such a beautiful whole who could not forgive him his quirks, those who truly loved him could and did and understood, sadly there were very few of those.
Elvis though everyone should try their hardest to be the best they could possibly be, perfectionists like him, he would try to encourage his friends to

give up their old ways and become more spiritual as he had done, and it upset him greatly that not only did they not try but they did not want to try, they were happy being the same as they had always been and they expected Elvis to be fine with that too, they even mocked him for his knowledge and powers until they needed Elvis's to help them or one of their family, then suddenly they believed in what he could do, but they never really got past their closed minds, which was a great disappointment, Elvis wanted to mentor everyone and share his knowledge and thought they were wasting their time boozing and gambling, he really had a hard time understanding this.

A lot of people have a very flat '1D' idea of who Elvis was, he was a good singer, and that is all they care about, but Elvis was so much more than that. Even people who supposedly knew Elvis like JD did not really know who Elvis was, I have heard him say in an interview that Elvis only listen to and sang gospel music at home, or he only read the bible, both are so untrue. Elvis had a very eclectic range of albums he listened to from Mario Lanza to Janis Joplin, ("Me and Bobby McGee" was one of his favourites,) and everything in between, and he sang them all in private. When Elvis was a child he loved reading British fairy stories, as a teen and into his early twenties he read medical journals, he said in an interview that used to be on YouTube, he read them in case he could help someone sometime, he would know what to do. A lot of people think Larry started Elvis on his quest for more spiritual knowledge, but this is not true. Since the age of seven when Vernon took Elvis in secret to see a comedy movie, Elvis knew the church they went to where everything that was fun was a sin was wrong. It was June Juanico who gave Elvis his first copy of the book 'The Prophet' in the 50s, not Larry. Elvis liked knowledge, he had an almost photographic mind, I have read his library had over a thousand books in it and Elvis had read them all, so people who say he only read the bible do not know Elvis at all. He liked all kinds of books, I had ones on colour therapy and ones on auras too, he loved anything 'new age', and anything ancient too, middle eastern, far eastern and most of all ancient American, he was passionate about the Mayans as his Mayan calendar suit shows, but not just the Mayans, the Olmecs, Toltecs and Incas and everything in between in Mesoamerica and South America, and all the indigenous north Americans, the Turtle Island people, those who were mound builders, Elvis wanted to know everything.

When I heard Linda had redecorated Graceland floor to ceiling in red, I knew it was her choice and not Elvis's, yet I have heard and read so many people blame Elvis for it and never has she owned up to it. Elvis knew all about colour therapy, what colours to use for different moods and what suited different rooms, he would never have chosen red everywhere like she did.

His curiosity and thirst for knowledge also made him a conspiracy theorist, he would sit for hours watching and rewatching the Kenndy assassination, was there a second gunman where did the bullet come from, when he was in the army, he was awarded for being an excellent marksman, so he would work out all the angles too. If there was something that did not sit right with him, he wanted to know why and he would delve into it until he had exhausted every possibility, so he was quite an accomplished conspiracy theorist about many things.

Elvis also believed in aliens, he read Von Daniken's "Chariots of Fire" as soon as it came out, he was a Trekkie and was trying to get a copy of Star Wars to watch when he was murdered, he liked the unknown, to try and work it all out, not only did he believe in aliens he would go into the desert when he was in Vegas to see if he could see any. This curiosity for the unknown also meant he was curious about vampires, and he met Vampira in 1956 when he first played Vegas, they booed him off the stage, she was in the audience, and sort him out to meet him, she thought him fantastic, he also coached a young Elvira after meeting her in Vegas in 68 and changed her life. This curiosity about the unknown also meant he liked to watch the films in the 70s like The Exorcist and The Omen. He also understood the British sense of humour and loved Monty Python. Nothing was off the table for Elvis if it existed, he wanted to know about it and even if it didn't really exist, he still wanted to know about it.

He also liked new inventions, anything that was unusual or got his curiosity going. Elvis had one of the first microwave ovens, and the first mobile phones, although you had to carry it around in a suitcase, he even had a TV in one of his cars, and a state-of-the-art security system in just about every room except his own rooms in Graceland, he could see and hear what anybody was doing at the flick of the switch. Someone said Elvis was a technophobe, do not believe it one second, if he were alive today he would have all the latest tech, and he would love social media, what better way to talk to all his friends from all over the world, when he was alive he would spend hours at the gates of his houses talking to fans, so social media would have been great for Elvis.

You can just see the TV screen behind his arm.

ELVIS TRIED TO BE LIKE JESUS

Elvis was spiritual not religious; he was a follower of Jesus. A lot of people find it hard to comprehend what this means. When Elvis was seven years old his daddy Vernon took him in secret to see a comedy movie, it had to be in secret because the church they belonged to preached anything that was fun was a sin, and it had to be in secret cause Gladys would have whopped them both had she found out. Right then at the tender age of seven Elvis knew the church and religion was wrong, because he knew what Jesus taught and he knew Jesus did not want everyone to be unhappy. So, Elvis started on his quest albeit in secret to be spiritual and not religious. Elvis knew what Jesus was, good and kind and humble and would help anyone he could, he knew Jesus did not distinguish one person from another to him all were equal, man and woman no matter what their race, and we should treat everyone the same and help them as in the story of the Good Samaritan. He also knew Jesus never judged anyone, let him who is without sin cast the first stone. All of these things made perfect sense to Elvis, and so he tried his best to be like Jesus. He knew religion divided people and the church often grew rich out of their suffering, that Jesus wanted everyone to be the same and that if religion really followed Jesus, it would not have all the different denominations all squabbling with each other over who best worshiped god, and sadly sometimes they even went to war over it, and Elvis knew no loving good God would want this. Neither would Jesus want the churches to be dripping in gold, jewels, and sacred objects while the people outside starved. Jesus always preached in the open and never inside he had said that nature was God's cathedral, and you would find him there, not in a temple.

So, Elvis tried as best he could to be like Jesus, to follow in his footsteps. Some people have accused me of putting Elvis on a pedestal of saying he was perfect, I know Elvis was not perfect, but he tried to be, in everything he did, it had to be the very best it could be, being good enough, was not being the best and being the best at what he did was what he always tried to be. Some people do not think Elvis was a good actor, but he was. When he was making some of those girly movies in the 60s he loathed them so much they made him physically ill to make them, as he himself said in an interview, but no one watching those movies would know it for one second because Elvis always did his best to be perfect, to give all he had to make sure it was the best it could be, he literally tried to make silk purses out of sows ears, so was Elvis perfect, no, but he always tried to be, which is what made him so good at everything he did and made him better than most, because he tried to be like Jesus, not just pay Jesus lip service like so many do. They proudly say they are

Christians and then do or say something totally against Jesus's teachings, I saw one say, they were nice to people who were nice to them, how is that being a Christian, Jesus said you should be nice to everyone, especially those who are not nice to you, for those you go the extra mile to try and include them in your flock, that person is not being the good shepherd that Jesus wanted us to be. Elvis understood this, so not only did he follow Jesus he also learnt about all the other religions and cultures of the world both current and ancient so he could better understand everyone on the planet, because like Jesus Elvis's greatest wish was to bring everyone together, had he of lived longer I think he might have managed it.

I know some people may not agree but Elvis's name is or was better known than anyone else by their first name and that included Jesus, why, because Elvis reached people in countries of all religions and into communist countries where the name of Jesus was never taught, in the early 60s people behind the iron curtain risked imprisonment to listen to Elvis in their basements and learned English so they knew what he was singing, that is how great Elvis's power was, the power of love, and his love transcended all cultures all over the world, in all countries people know who Elvis is, there are Elvis impersonators in just about every country on the planet, and yet this man died over 45 years ago, who else could make such an impression in today's world, there have been books written about all those he helped in their darkest hour, not only while he was alive but since his death, his love, his goodness, shines on even now and brings people from everywhere together, that is how great Elvis still is, was he perfect, no, but he was as perfect as a man could be given his circumstances and it was that vision he had, that love he gave unconditionally to everyone that is why he is still remember today.

Elvis strove to be like Jesus in every way he could and he did it well, he did it as perfectly as he could and that is why you can find things like this, that people who are neither American, because Elvis's appeal was worldwide, and are not Christian, because Elvis transcended all beliefs by being as pure in heart as he could be, and by learning everything he could about everyone one and everything.

May 21, 1996, Web posted at: 6:15 p.m. EDT (2215 GMT) NEW DELHI, India (CNN) – '' In one small town in the Indian state of Karnataka, a picture of Elvis Presley hangs beside  pictures of Hindu gods in a temple, according to a report in India Today magazine''. This is a testimony to how great Elvis was and is because as a small boy he to follow Jesus, to become spiritual, not religious.

ELVIS WAS SPIRITUAL NOT RELIGIOUS

Firstly, let this sink in for a moment, if Elvis had not become spiritual and had stuck to the teachings of the church he grew up in, we would never have known him, the world would never have known him.

It's one of the reasons why this is so important. Elvis once said he thought he would be forgotten about within two years of his death, but the truth is many 'fans' have never accepted who Elvis really was, they are only interested in the image and the music, some even relish in the lies told about him, they do not want to know who Elvis really was, so in a way Elvis was right, which is so sad.

Some people think of him as Christian because of the church he was brought up in, but Elvis hated the way the church he was brought up in made you feel, that everything that was fun was a sin, his daddy took him to see a movie when he was 7, in secret, and did not tell Gladys cause it was against their churches doctrine, Elvis could not understand how something so entertaining which made you happy was a sin.

He was convinced there was a better way and Jesus would not want people to be miserable all the time. So even at an early age he was more spiritual than religious. Others think he is Jewish because he wore a chia in his last year and there is Jewish blood on his mother's side. Although he was born in Tupelo, he considered Memphis to be his home, coincidentally Memphis was the name of the capital of ancient Egypt, and todays Memphis even has a pyramid and Elvis often wore an ankh at one point and had many jumpsuits reflecting his love of ancient Egypt. Elvis knew there was more than what the bible holds, he knew the New Testament was compiled for a Roman emperor who had his own political agenda, he knew about the dead sea scrolls and the gnostic gospels and that many gospels including Peters and even Jesus's were left out because they did not fit in with Constantine's political agenda.

Elvis was more spiritual than religious and some of the things Elvis believed would have got him shunned from church. Elvis was a very complex spiritual man who sought out all manner of different religions, philosophies, and mystic teachings from all over the world. At one time in the 60s Elvis considered becoming a monk so he could dedicate himself to his spiritual side. He believed in many things, he used numerology extensively, and astrology. He believed in reincarnation, and that he was a very old soul. He had supernatural abilities; he was a healer and could control the rain. He was an empath, he was psychic, telekinetic, and telepathic, he could lucid-dream and he could astral travel, and he knew about the akashic record. If he had of had longer to continue his path of enlightenment, he could have easily become a seer or prophet, but he knew many of his fans and people he knew were not ready for this side of his personality and had had many battles because of it with so-called friends and his manager and ex-wife, also do not forget at the beginning of his career how the church tried to have him banned, they called him the devil and other such ridiculous things, so Elvis also knew what damage closed-minded religion could do.

To pigeonhole Elvis to one religion is doing him a great dis-service and injustice, his spirituality was very complex, deep, and all-encompassing of everything and the older he got the more his thirst for all knowledge grew and became much greater. The last book he was reading was "Sex And Psychic Energy" by Betty Bethards, showing again his understanding of telepathy and meditation. Elvis was and is a free spirit, for Elvis god and Jesus are a universal power for good and love who belonged to all not just one religion.

Elvis believed in reincarnation, he believed in many things and whether you believe in them or not that does not matter, when a loved one believes in something you try and understand you do not judge and criticize. Many of Elvis's friends witnessed him using his special powers, even Marty talks about Elvis astral traveling, and most witnessed him control the rain or use his healing hands on them, even now a lot of people feel his presence his spirit.

There is absolutely no reason to ridicule, it is no surprise Elvis kept his believes secret when even now pious people scoff and laugh at him, even Elvis himself said: "People think you're crazy if you talk about things they don't understand." we all know Elvis believed in many 'alternative things', and one of those things was reincarnation.

In Ginger Alden's book it says Elvis told her he thought he was once a holy master called Koot Hoomi. Elvis also admired David Andria's book through the eyes of the masters, which expounded on the belief that a person could reincarnate in another person's body. Over time, Elvis would tell Ginger he thought Koot Hoomi, one of the masters from the book, was incarnated in himself, and pointed out a photo with the master dressed in a high-collared jacket similar to his own favourite style at the time. Elvis felt there was some force inside him, guiding him to teach and bring joy to others in various ways, especially through music. He was reading these books not only to understand his own life but to help others as well. And this about Koot Hoomi from wiki, Koot Hoomi is said to be one of the mahatmas that inspired the founding of the theosophical society. He engaged in correspondence with two English theosophists living in India, a. P. Sinnett and a. O. Hume, in which correspondence was published in the book the Mahatma letters to a. P. Sinnett.

Elvis also believed he was Jesus reincarnated he saw the similarities between their lives, he even called the MMs his disciples and Elvis tried to live with the same principles as Jesus did, as he did when he was Jesus.

So please try and remember all of whom Elvis was, because a singer is just a small part of who he was.

CHAPTER TWO

Elvis's quote

"TRUTH IS LIKE THE SUN.
YOU CAN SHUT IT OUT FOR A
TIME,
BUT IT AIN'T GOING AWAY"

Scare tactics.

I have on several occasions been threatened with being sued, because of my Facebook Elvis page, though I never have been, for retelling things that have been told to me, or that I have read, or indeed because I pointed out a lie they themselves have said, of course they won't sue because then the truth would come out and people would realise how much these people lie to make themselves look good and Elvis bad. It always amazes me that people can tell as many untruths about Elvis as they like, and no one bats an eyelid.

GRACELAND

Anybody remember Paul Harvey's "The Rest Of The Story" broadcasts? Well, we need one here, because too many people are willing to let Priscilla claim all the credit for Graceland being opened to the public and praise her business acumen for making it a success when she really had little to do with it. While Priscilla stayed in Los Angeles pretending to be an actress, the Tennessee courts appointed Memphis attorneys to protect Lisa's interests because she was a minor, which is standard procedure in any state.

Tennessee law requires that most cemeteries on private property provide some public access, particularly for descendants, those doing academic research, and graves of historically significant people. That access only has to be reasonable, not all day, but at least part of the day. That's why Vernon let fans walk up each day, and why EPE continues the morning walk-ups still, it's not because they want to, but they have no choice, it was part of the agreement to get approval to bury the bodies on the property, making Graceland a cemetery.

While doing inventory of the estate, the trustees, Lisa's lawyers, and their staff noticed the number of fans from all over the world visiting the graves each morning and wondered if the house could generate income as a museum. The city of Memphis had already approached Vernon about buying Graceland and turning it into a museum but could only pay $600,000. That offer was rejected but the city may have gotten somewhere if Vernon hadn't died. The trustees, Priscilla then becoming one of several, contacted people with backgrounds in museum and theme park operations, including Jack Soden and his business partner, who not long after was killed in a plane crash, and plans to open Graceland developed from there.

So it wasn't because of Priscilla, nor Lisa, nor Vernon, but you can thank the excellent lawyers the court-appointed for Lisa, the trustees from the bank named in Elvis' will, and the fans who walked up to visit Elvis' grave when that was all they could do, for saving Graceland. The court had to approve the plan as being in Lisa's best interest because she was still a minor. Priscilla, as Lisa's guardian and trustee certainly had input, but in fact, her consent was not needed. All she had to do was sit back in California and watch the money start rolling in. And as an aside, the probate court valued Elvis' estate at $7.6 million, which is the equivalent today of between $30 - $40 million, so while the estate may have been cash-poor initially, there were assets there to help ensure that Lisa wasn't left penniless. If it had been left to Cilla the estate would have become bankrupt and would have had to have been sold, because she allowed Parker to carry mismanaging the finances. These facts from Wiki;   By 1980, the cost of running the estate was estimated to be as much as $500,000 a year.[2] Priscilla and the Trust were prepared to let Parker continue to handle Presley's business affairs, and petitioned the court to that end.[3] However, Judge Joseph Evans, aware that Lisa Marie Presley was still a minor, appointed attorney Blanchard E. Tual to investigate Parker's management. [2][3] Tual, once appointed as Lisa Marie's guardian ad litem, chose to investigate the entire period of Parker's management of Presley; his preliminary finding was that Parker's management deal of 50% was extortionate compared to the industry average of 15–20%.[2] He also noted that Parker's handling of Presley's business affairs during his lifetime, including the decision to sell off past royalties to RCA for $5.4 million in 1973, was "unethical" and poorly handled.[3] During a second, more detailed investigation, Tual discovered that all earnings were paid directly to the Trust instead of Parker.[2] By this time, with the IRS demanding almost $15 million in taxes, the estate was facing bankruptcy.[2] On August 14, 1981, Judge Evans ordered EPE to sue Parker for mismanagement.[3] In response to this, Parker countersued.[3] The case against Parker was settled out of court in 1983, with the estate paying him $2 million (US$5,196,793 in 2020 dollars[9])[3] in exchange for all Presley audio recordings or visual images that he owned[2] and the termination of his involvement in any Presley related earnings for five years.[2]

PARKER

Most of us think of Parker as the greedy
shabbily dressed man but was he a little fish in a
big pond, or one of the sharks at the top.
Parker went to America as an illegal immigrant
when he was 20 in 1929, he left Breda where he
was wanted for murder. In America he took on
the name of Tom Parker, the person who
interviewed him to join the army in
approximately 1930 and after two years went
AWOL and when they got him, they put him in a
psychiatric ward, and he was discharged from
the army because he was a psychopath. Now to
be deemed a psychopath back then was quite
unusual and was usually reserved for the worst
of the worst, not like today when we know that
many psychopaths lead a seemingly normal life
and never get into trouble, but then it was
unusual, what he did doesn't seem clear.

In the early 50 he became a music promoter,
now through all this from what I have read it is
not clear how he obtained illegal papers, just
that he had them, was it then that the mob
became interested in him? What we do know is
by the time he became Elvis's manager he was

ensconced with the mob, and suddenly had 'friends' in high places, and I am sure got a nice bonus for selling Elvis to the mob. Before Elvis went to Germany there was a notice in a newspaper telling Elvis to be careful in Germany or he would be coming home needing dental treatment according to Elaine Dundy's book "Elvis and Gladys" she writes about an article with mob undertones warning Elvis to keep his mouth shut and not to do or say anything he should not, she says the article in Billboard magazine said that "High on Presley's agenda, is extensive dental and periodontal (gum) work" but there was nothing wrong with Elvis's teeth, this apparently is mafia/mob code for keeping your mouth shut. When Elvis was in Germany, they put him on the big guns and when he went home that night, he could not hear, Lamar Fike got on the phone straight away to Parker in America who, Lamar says phoned his friend in the Pentagon and quicky had Elvis reassigned. Could you imagine Elvis coming home partially deaf, his singing career over. I have often said that Elvis did not want to get drafted, and that Parker had plenty of reasons to get his draft withdrawn, Elvis was an only child and the breadwinner of not only his immediate his family, but his great family too, and his mother was gravely ill, which in peacetime is usually enough.

Fike said: - "Elvis was a tank gunner. which I guess, looking back, was a pretty appropriate assignment. Elvis loved guns, and these were big guns. but there was a problem because those guns were loud, and one day Elvis came home, and I asked him how it went that day, and he walked right on past me. I followed him into the bedroom and said, "hey, didn't you hear me?" "what are you talking about?" Elvis answered, and I realized he hadn't heard a word I'd said. I asked him if he was all right and he said, "my ears are ringing so loud I can't even hear". I immediately got Colonel Parker on the phone in the states and told him we had a problem, a big problem. Colonel Tom knew a guy at the Pentagon, and he just wore this man's butt out until they reassigned Elvis out of that damned tank". To me this says not only had Parker climbed the ranks of the mob very quickly because of his prize cash-cow, but the mob was also in the Pentagon and could throw orders around.

Years later there is also this, we know Fike was on Parkers payroll because of the story of getting 'Change of Habit' to Elvis, someone I used to know told me a story of how she was charged with getting "Change of Habit" to Elvis, she had known Elvis in the early day and had been a fan club president, she was now working for New York for MCA/Universal and because of her previous connection to Elvis they tasked her with the job of getting the story to him, she knew Tom Diskin, and so contacted him and asked if he could get her to see Elvis on a personal matter, two days later Elvis phones her and she explained about the story to him and he asked her to go to Los Angeles, and he said he would have someone to pick her up at the airport, that someone was Fike, who drove her around and around eventually he made an excuse and said he could not take her to Elvis's house, Fike told her to give him the script and he would give it to Elvis and he would take her to her hotel, she refused, she had a feeling something was not right, Fike eventually took her to her hotel and she phoned her boss, who phoned Lou Wasserman the President Of Universal who called someone big at MGM, next morning there was a car to take her straight to the studio where Elvis was making 'Live A Little Love a Little', after a little while someone went to get Elvis from his trailer and they chatted a while and she handed Elvis the script. She told me Elvis asked her what happened the day before that he had sent someone to pick her up, not wanting to sound crazy and perhaps get Fike into trouble, she said her flight was late. Fike had done all he could to stop the script from getting to Elvis, all we can assume is it was on Parkers orders as Parker wanted to control everything and did not want an unvetted script getting to Elvis, as it happened the original script she took to Elvis was changed so much by

Parker and his people it was hardly recognisable by the time Elvis made the film.

Parker did not care about how Elvis felt at all about the movies he had him make, all he cared about was how much money they could make and how fast they could be made, even though making them made Elvis physically and emotionally unwell, and most of the films Elvis was in Parker made sure there was a sly dig in there against Elvis in some way to let him know who was boss, Elvis almost fired Parker over Jailhouse Rock, because Parker was mocking Elvis's family, but Gladys told Elvis to do whatever Parker wanted so he did not reveal to the world about the family secret that Vernon had spent time in jail and so the dye was set and poor Elvis always obeyed his mother, right until he was almost in his forties, only then did he put his foot down with Parker. In Roustabout Parker made Elvis do several wardrobe shots in dungarees though never was there going to be a scene where he would wear them, knowing how Elvis hated the garment, in Easy come Easy Go, Parker made a mockery of Elvis's believes in meditation and yoga with the pretzel song, although Elvis was extremely good at yoga and even wanted to become a Buddhist Monk at one time, because Parker hated Larrys influence on Elvis although it was June Juanico who actually gave Elvis his first book about it, "The Prophet", Larry was just the first person who understood, do you know not only did Parker forbid Larry from seeing Elvis in the late 60s he had his goons ransack his home with the warning this time it was when your family were not there next time they will be. In 'Double Trouble' they go on and on about the girl being underage, but in fact she was not because the film was supposed to be in Europe and she was supposed to be English where the age of consent is 16 and in fact in a lot of Europe then it was younger, again having a dig at Elvis because of Cillas age when Elvis met her and the fact they still were not married when it was filmed. PARKER was a leech with a noose around Elvis's neck.

In the horrible lying book that the Wests did they sing Parker praises, why, I think it was just part of the greater conspiracy of Elvis's murder and they too were in Parkers employ. In Darrin Lee's book Elvis & Alicia, he states the Wests book was financed by Star tabloid owner Rupert Murdoch & they received a $125k advance. I think the so called CBS Special was also part of the bigger cover-up orchestrated by Parker, everyone who saw Elvis at those shows and other shows on that tour have told me that they chose the very worst bits to put in the special, that Elvis was in no way as bloated and unwell as the show made out and that Elvis was on top form for the whole of the tour, which can be seen in the amateur video of the very last concert on the 26th of June 1977 in Indianapolis and all the stills from that concert, Elvis looks great and sounded great, but the world was told the CBS show was Elvis's last concert when it was not, and all they see is someone who has been made to look ill, so when Elvis did die just over six weeks later, very few raised an eyebrow, that together with the book the world just thought another junkie come to the end of his life, and even the person who let the EMTs into Graceland said they thought Elvis had over dosed, now no one would ever have said that who was in only Elvis's employ, only someone who wanted Elvis to look bad. Before Elvis was cold in his grave Parker was hounding Vernon to sign all of Elvis's business over to him and let us not forget how this heartless person with no respect for Elvis turned up dressed at Elvis's funeral.

After Elvis died and it became known that Parker was illegal and wanted for murder, why was he not turned over to Interpol as anyone else would have been, don't forget his friends in the Pentagon, and even more so why is it that Cilla still sings his praises even though Parker lost her, 'Lisas estate' millions, Cilla sues people at the drop of a hat, but even now she is still singing Parkers praises, Tom Hanks said he was amazed when he asked Cilla about Parker how much she praised him. To me there can only be one answer Cilla knew the plan and that she to is afraid to say anything negative about him in case it comes back on her. I do not think Parker was a poor little fish with a gambling habit at all. I think he became one of the sharks at the top of the pond and could get away with anything he wanted, murder in Breda and murder in Memphis, and something that always bothered me why were the police and everyone else on high alter in case there was rioting if Elvis's death had been found not to be natural, why was that suspicion there, there must have been a good reason, like Elvis was murdered and it was covered up quickly to stop the carnage that might have followed.

https://www.smithsonianmag.com/history/colonel-parker-managed-elvis-career-but-was-he-a-killer-on-the-lam-108042206/

https://en.wikipedia.org/wiki/Colonel_Tom_Parker

THE FIRED THREE

This from a Memphis resident
It has always surprised me that most Memphians know the reason while fans outside of Memphis never had a clue. First off, Bill Morris was the sheriff of Shelby County from 1964 to 1970 then elected Mayor in 1978. Bill carried a lot of political weight and he and Elvis were close friends. In fact, I'd imagine Elvis discussed things with Bill he would never discuss with anyone else. The Graceland property is not surrounded by the rock wall fans are familiar with. In some areas there is privacy

fence while in other areas there is only the chain link variety. Fans were always finding their way onto the Graceland grounds. These were fans that just wanted a peek, a snapshot, maybe an autograph and we're just a bit overzealous. They didn't mean Elvis any harm. Realizing this Elvis' instructions to the security staff was simple... they were to politely escort them from the property and if Vester or Travis were there that's what would occur.

Red, Sonny, and Dave also were apart of Elvis' security detail and responsible for the grounds when Elvis was home, usually in the evening time. The three rarely followed Elvis' orders and would escort trespassers off the property after giving the offenders a good beating. This usually resulted in Elvis being sued which happened quite a bit in the 70's. One evening in early to mid-76 Red caught a guy on the back property with a camera and a telephoto lens. Red and Sonny beat the guy senseless, and he was thrown out the front gate in front of some fans that had gathered. By this time Hebler had joined the other two. One young man in the crowd, a 16-year-old was offended at what he had just witnessed and told Red what he thought. Red then hit the kid in the mouth and after he fell Hebler kicked him in the ribs. What they didn't know was that they had just assaulted Bill Morris' grandson. The kid had a date with a foreign exchange student who wanted to see Graceland. Two evenings later Mr. Morris had a private meeting with Elvis and Vernon where Morris explained to Elvis that if any of his people attached another citizen without probable cause he would personally see to it that charges were filed, and he would see to it that those charges stuck, all friendships aside, the camel's back was broken. Morris also pointed out the publicity something like this would bring would be devastating to Elvis. Morris, I understand pointed out that Red, Sonny, and Dave were embarrassments to Elvis, the good people of Memphis and Shelby County not to mention the laws of the state and their behaviour wouldn't be tolerated any longer and they couldn't hide behind Elvis any longer. Elvis was hopping mad because no one had told him what had happened a couple nights before. Vernon convinced Elvis to go to Palm Springs or Denver, I can't recall which and cool off...he'd handle it and that he did. Now I know there will be some fans that have never been to Memphis but have read all the tabloids and want to argue with me, but it doesn't change the fact that this is exactly what happened. Of course, these two assaults cost Elvis quite a bit of money and I think the terms of settlement included that details of the assaults would not be made public but there were fans at the gate that night and news travels quickly and the walls in Vernon office definitely had ears.

DAVE HEBLER

Dave Hebler would have you believe that there was one maybe two fights with fans, he always underplays what happened, now either he is lying, or Elvis is, and you know who my money is on, read carefully what Elvis says, **"there were six lawsuits in two years."**, not one or two, six.

These are Elvis's words extracted from the telephone call Red West made to Elvis, the transcript can be found online and at the end of their horrible lying book, all I have done is put the words Elvis spoke about Dave Hebler together as one instead of throughout the conversation, and not once did Red say to Elvis he was wrong about Dave Hebler: -

VARIETY

Wednesday, June 11, 1975

Sues Presley For 30G Over Alleged Beating In Vegas

Carson City, Nev., June 10.
Elvis Presley and others are being sued in Carson District Court by a man who charges he was severely beaten by one of the singer's bodyguards during a September, 1973 incident at the Las Vegas Hilton.

Keijo Peter Pajarinen claims he was attacked by bodyguard Bobby G. "Red" West after he voluntarily agreed to leave a Sept. 7 party at Presley's 30th floor Hilton suite. Once outside the suite, Pajarinen claims he was "suddenly, viciously and maliciously attacked without provocation by West." He asserts West was wearing brass knuckles—and Pajarinen suffered a broken nose and other injuries.

Pajarinen contends Presley was negligent in hiring and retaining West since he was aware of the latter's vicious propensities" and of the fact that he had, allegedly, "committed unprovoked attacks on other persons in the guise of protecting him."

Also named in the suit, in which Pajarinen is asking in excess of $30,000 damages, are two other unnamed Presley bodyguards, the Hilton Hotel Corp., five unnamed "Does," and the "Black and White Corp."

Presley also is a defendant in a $5,000,000 suit, filed last August in Federal Court in Reno, by Edward Ashley, a Grass Valley, Calif., man. According to the complaint, he was beaten by a Presley bodyguard at the Sahara Tahoe Hotel at Stateline when he tried to gain admittance to a party in the singer's suite.

*"I was wrong about Hebler. just a bad thing on my part. he was very undermining and sneaky. he hated all you guys and everybody else and I kept this ****. it just burned into my ear.... and those god damn lawsuits, you know how those lawyers are, there were six lawsuits in two years.*

I was very disillusioned about Hebler. he faked me off something terrible.
he would say things to me, who he hated. Ed Parker told me, keep him at arm's length. this went on over a period of over two years, it's hard to explain. I don't think he liked anyone in the group. I think I became a dollar sign to him. Hebler tried to bully his way through everything with scare tactics with some of these young guys. they would ask a question like and never get a straight answer, they were turned down at every corner. I just felt I should talk to you and let you see my side of it".

Dave Hebler work for Elvis for approximately two years, before he went to work for Elvis it is my understanding there had never been trouble like this with fans getting beaten up and lawsuits, only after Hebler started to work for Elvis. Hebler also seems to know little about the man he worked for as it has come to my attention he claimed Elvis never had after show parties, when there is plenty of photo evidence to prove the contrary, Hebler also told someone who spoke to me that Hebler said Elvis was rubbish at karate and said the Alice Cooper incident could never have happened, the fact is it did, and I would also like to remind people that Elvis was so quick that he took the legs out from under Muhammad Ali on first meeting who became a good friend of Elvis's. This to me shows just how little Hebler knew Elvis even though he has made himself a spokesman for Elvis a man who clearly did not like or trust Hebler at all, as I said at the beginning, I know who's word I would believe, and it would not be Hebler's.

THE GREAT DIAMOND HEIST

This is about a story in Dr Nicks book, I wanted to tell it because it shows none of those in the backing group were loyal to Elvis, it was about the money and maybe the prestige.
The story goes like this, Elvis told everyone to be at the airport at a certain time to fly to the next destination for the next concert, instead of going straight to the airport or informing Elvis of their plans they all decided to go for something to eat first, saying that Elvis was hardly ever on time, so they thought they would have plenty of time, but Elvis was on time and after waiting about half an hour he told the pilot to take off. Just then the group of people got to the runway in time to see the jet flying off into the distance, now Elvis had no plans to leave them stranded

and turned around and went back to get them, Elvis wanted to make a point. He was the boss, something that seemed to be lost on most of them. The next day they all told Elvis they were on strike because of what he had done. So, Elvis phoned his jeweller Lowell and Hays and asked him to get there as quick as possible with his case of jewellery, he then told everyone they could pick whatever they wanted as long as they played that night, and of course they did. For me this is so wrong on so many levels, it shows they had no respect for Elvis as their boss or even a man like they all profess to have, they knew how scared Elvis was of going on stage by himself, how he would literally get frozen with stage fright, and they used his insecurities against him like it seems most people in his life did, to my knowledge none of them stood up for Elvis and said they would go on stage with him. We know for the audience only Elvis mattered and if he went on stage alone with his guitar the audience would still be screaming and be in his thrall, they also all must have known the financial difficulty Elvis was in because of the divorce and other things, but they did not care about Elvis they cared about themselves and their greed, so when they all say how much they loved him and respected him, remind them of this and ask them why they did not stand by his side and tell him he did not need any of them, that he was the star, not them.

This is a story that Marty Lacker tells, he said one day he called out to Elvis that he wanted a word and before he had chance to say anything else, Elvis said, "how much", so used was Elvis to having people asking him for money, but Marty did not want money, he wanted to pay Elvis back some money he had given (loaned) him, Elvis was so overwhelmed someone actually wanted to pay him back because it had never happened before as far as Marty knew, Elvis started to cry. I think this story shows just how used Elvis was to being used constantly by those who were supposed to be his friends, and I think he also knew deep down the only reason why some stayed was because it was easy money and plenty of perks for them. Elvis knew most of their friendship had been bought, not all of them of course but quite a few. Otherwise, Elvis would not have got so touched that someone actually respected him enough to want to pay him back.

JOE ESPOSITO

Many people believe Joe was Elvis's best friend, but why? Someone who knew Elvis in the 50s once told me it was common knowledge back then that it was Joe who first gave Elvis pills to help him stay awake all night while doing guard duty in the army. When Elvis returned from

Germany in 1960 both Joe and Charlie who Elvis had met in the army became employed by Elvis, Joes was paid according to Google $65 a week, in 1960 that was a lot of money, today it would be the equivalent of about $666 for one weeks work. In the 60s Elvis fired Joe because Joe reported back to Parker everything Elvis told him or that he had heard, Elvis was furious, even his personal and private stuff, for Elvis, Parker was business and the less he knew about Elvis's private life the better, as Parker had a long history of using anything he could against Elvis to manipulate him into doing what Parker wanted. Now the official story is a while after being fired Joe went crawling back to Elvis begging for his job back with a sob-story about being on the breadline, why I have no idea, surely he could have got another job if he had tried, unofficially it is said Parker ordered Elvis to take his spy back on the books. In the MMs book they make it quite clear that Joe was not part of the gang, they say he was always pushing himself to the front for the limelight, that Joe was friends with Cilla and Jerry, but he looked down on the rest of them. Now you would think Joe would have learnt his lesson, but he carried on as if nothing had happened, and continued reporting everything back to Parker. When Elvis went back on the road touring, Joe was made tour manager, the relationship between Elvis and Joe became more fraught as the 70s carried on. One of Joe's jobs was to lead Elvis off the stage and to his waiting vehicle, because of the glaucoma Elvis found his eyes took a long time to adjust from the blinding stage lights to the dimly lit backstage areas. One time I have read as Joe was leading Elvis down some stairs Joe saw something going on and left Elvis to go and see what was happening, Elvis slipped and twisted his ankle, Elvis was furious it has been said, understandably it could have cost Elvis and everyone a lot of money had Elvis had to cancel the next concerts because of it. Joe was starting to act more like he was the boss, not Elvis, even refusing to contact someone one night for Elvis. Joe was also suing Elvis over the racquetball courts debacle, friends do not sue friends and they do not put friends in the position Joe and others put Elvis in, they all seemed to think Elvis was made of money but he was not, he worked hard for his money and had to carry on working when he wanted to retire to pay all the people he felt responsible for, and Joe was one of those people. By the time Elvis died, Joe who was, I have read the highest paid, was earning $40,000 plus bonuses and a car, and yet he still cried poverty to Elvis, today that would be the equivalent of around $230,000 which is a lot of money, especially considering it was only when Elvis was on tour. So, no Joe was not Elvis's best friend at all in my estimation.

ED PARKER AND THE LAS VEGAS DRUGGING

A lot of people like Ed Parker, they will tell you he really loved Elvis, as far as I am concerned he used his 'friendship' with Elvis as kudos as so many others did, firstly a story that you can check out on-line, and then a story you cannot, but I wanted to show you the sort of person he was and the calibre of the people Elvis had surrounding him.

In 1973 accompanied by Linda and some friends Elvis flew to San Francisco, to attend Ed Parker's California Karate Championships. There he discovered the unauthorized use of his name both in promotion and on the marquee and so Elvis flew straight back to Los Angeles again, very disappointed about this exploitation by his 'friend', if he had asked, Elvis would have probably been glad to allow his friend to use his name, but most of them were so used to getting what they wanted when they wanted from Elvis that asking permission was something they forgot about.

A few years after Elvis's death in 1980, it was Ed according to Ginger who got her the part in the horrible movie "Living Legend, the King of Rock and Roll", Ginger claims she had no idea the movie was about Elvis, which I find very hard to believe. I am sure Ed got a nice commission for it though. So, this tells you Ed was not an honourable man, he used Elvis the same as most of the rest did and you can check those dates if you want to.

Here is a story told to me a few years back by one of the super fans. It goes to show how little those around Elvis thought of Elvis, that they were there to enjoy themselves and what being Elvis's 'friend' could do for them. This was told to me by a fan who knew Elvis, the fan told me Elvis asked her up to his suite after a show, she said they went upstairs together, that Elvis was in good spirits and happy with the show he had done and she was looking forward to spending some time with him, keeping him company as a friend as he hated being alone. When they got to his room Ed Parker and Dr Ghanem were waiting for Elvis, so Elvis told the girl to wait there while he found out what the guys wanted, and he would be back out in a minute for her. The three of them went into the room and someone closed the door, she said she then heard a scuffle and Dr Ghanem, and Ed opened the door and dragged an unconscious Elvis down the corridor, when she asked them what had happened, they said he had to be tranquilised for his own good. She knew this was garbage as he was in a really good and pleasant mood, not upset at all, so when she saw one of the other guys, she asked them about what she had witnessed and he told her, it's just easier than having someone sitting there watching him all night in case he sleepwalks so they sedate him.

Now I am sure when he woke, they convinced Elvis it was for his own good, but it was not, it was so they could go and party instead of doing what they were paid for, which was looking after Elvis. I cannot remember exactly when this took place, except of course it was in the 70s, but these are the sort of people whose hands that Elvis's life was in, they did not care about Elvis only what being part of the gang could do for them and their celebrity status.

I understand Elvis being drugged against his will is in two other books as well, in one of David Stanley's books and in "Blue Star Love: From an Amazing Heart of Grace" by Maia Chrystine Nartoomid. So, I have no course to doubt the person who told me about it.

ICE BUCKET MYTH

There are many stories about Elvis that have a hint of truth and a lot of things made up either to sell books or because people with wild imaginations are telling the stories, and the one about the ice bucket is one of them. What is most frustrating and sad about this kind of thing is that if people would use their own common sense, they realise just how far fetched these types of myths are.

THE MYTH
The myth goes Elvis had a raging temperature,
so high he lost consciousness and Parker raged
that Dr Nick had to get Elvis on stage that night
at any cost and Dr Nick held Elvis's head into a
bucket of ice till he recovered, some also add to
the story that the bucket of ice-water had an
astringent smell to it, the thing is none of those
who tell the story where in the room when it
happened they were outside, and were only
allowed in afterwards, like typical of some
people they put 2 and 2 together and came up
with 22 instead of 4, so if you have heard this
myth, it DID NOT HAPPEN LIKE THAT AT ALL,
I will tell you what did happen and why this myth
is impossible to be true, and if you use your
mind and knowledge of how the human body
works you would know it not to be true, but the
truth is not as sensational as the myth.

WHAT REALLY HAPPENED

This is a shortened version, but this is it, Vernon
had called Dr Nick concerned for Elvis's health,
so when he got to the hotel he enquired with the
guys where Elvis was and they said they had not
seen him, so Dr Nick went to Elvis's room
unable to get him to answer he got Joe to use
his spare key. Dr Nick says it was one of the
scariest times he ever had, Elvis was fading in
and out of consciousness and Elvis was red hot,
and still in his PJs on the bed, from his condition

Dr Nick thought he had had a seizure, possibly brought on by an anti-depressant Elvis had been taking. Dr Nick and Joe took Elvis's clothing off him and dragged his limp body into the bathroom and put him into a cold bath, and Dr Nick says he worked on him till he slowly started to come round, they then got him out of the bath and back on to his bed and put some clothes on him. It is at this stage Parker starts hammering on the door demanding Elvis be on stage that night. Obviously, someone had told him there was something wrong with Elvis, and this is also when the rest of the entourage saw into the room and as I said I think they added 2+2 together and came up with 22.

Firstly, if you put someone's head, who is unconscious as Elvis was, in water, even a bucket of ice water, they will drown, they will breathe in the water and drown, many people have been knocked unconscious and fallen into water and drowned, because the body carries on breathing, not aware of what it is breathing. So, no way did Dr Nick or anyone hold Elvis's head when he was unconscious forcibly into a bucket of ice water. I think although Dr Nick does not say it in his book he had Joe get a bucket of ice water to swab Elvis with and to cool the bath down quicker, as for the astringent some say was in the bucket of ice water I think and again it is my assumption, but an assumption based on logic and knowledge, that Dr Nick quite possibly used what used to be called smelling salts to help bring Elvis around, doctors have little snap packs with ammonia in them, once used they are discarded and I think that is what Dr Nick used and discarded into the then half full bucket of ice water that was no longer needed.

So, the MMs come in and see Elvis with wet hair, after Parkers ranting, and see a bucket half filled with ice water and Elvis's eyes bloodshot because of the high temperature he had, and they came to the wrong conclusions. Also, never would Dr Nick put an astringent near Elvis eyes because of the glaucoma. So next time you read

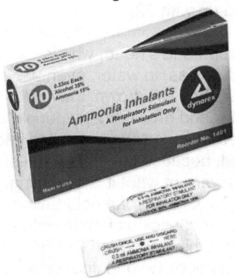

the ice bucket story somewhere know that it is mostly fiction. source: - Dr Nicks book page 52

I believe this is the type of thing that was used and why some said the water smelt astringent because it had been dropped as waste into the bucket.

MYTH BUSTED

COLOURBLIND

There are two myths in particular about this subject and both are completely wrong. The first started when someone accused Elvis of saying that the only use he had for blacks was to shine his shoes, but where this was supposed to have been said, and when, Elvis was not even in that place at the time it was supposed to have occurred and those who know Elvis know he would never have thought it let alone said it, the other myth is that he stole black music, which is as ridiculous as the first accusation.

Everyone who knew Elvis said he was colourblind, meaning he never saw a person's colour, I have already related one story about him sharing his ice-cream with a black child when he himself was a child, but to show it was not just as a child he never saw a person's colour, here is another story. Elvis always had black backing singers in his later career and when he was due to do a concert in Texas, they told him to get other backing singers, they didn't want his black backing singers, Elvis immediately told them if his backing singers were not welcome then he was not going to Texas, of course they had to recant. When one of his black backing singers learned she had cancer it was Elvis who asked what was wrong, when she told him he sat there all-night healing her, in the morning when she saw the doctor the tumour had miraculously gone, now believe in healing or not, Elvis would not have sat there all night with her if he had not liked blacks. Elvis also dated a coloured girl who worked at Graceland for a few months as well.

Elvis had many black friends, some in the business others not, the list is quite long but here are a few you will all know: - B.B. King, Jackie Wilson, Elvis met both of these early on in his career and remained good friends with them. When Jackie had a heart attack in the 70s it was Elvis who paid his hospital bills till Elvis himself died. When Elvis died James Brown who called Elvis his soul brother had to be lead away from Elvis's coffin after about twenty minutes still sobbing at the loss of his friend. Fats Domino was also a good friend of Elvis's and was at the 69-press conference with him as was Sammy Davis Jr, who knew Elvis from almost the beginning and said he was his brother also. Muhammad Ali was also a good friend of Elvis's, he said Elvis was the nicest man he had ever met, and when Elvis needed to get away from it all he would go to Ali's training camp in the woods and stay in one of the cabins there. These people would not have been friends with Elvis if he had been at all prejudice in any way, and far from accusing him of stealing their music, they acknowledge it was Elvis who opened doors for them and allowed them to become famous. Do not forget when Elvis first started out white radio stations would not play his records because he sounded black and black stations would not play him because he was white, now tell me who were the prejudice ones were, certainly not Elvis.

MYTH BUSTED.

Elvis with Jackie Wilson

PRISCILLAS MYTHS

I personally think Priscilla often says the first thing that comes into her head that she thinks will either excuse her behaviour or will get the fans sympathy, she then often recants what she has said a few years down the line when she realises that the public and fans either do not believe her or the myth/lie does not serve her anymore.

THE RAPE MYTH/LIE

Sometime after Elvis died Cilla decided to write a book and had a TVM made of it, one of the worst possible things she ever said was in that book, that Elvis had raped her, in the TVM it was even worse as you saw what has been described as Elvis violently rapping her, as usual they never seem to hear Cilla recant, she said it was all a misunderstanding and Elvis never rapped her. I think is Cilla was looking for sympathy when she wrote the book and when the fans did not like what they read and more over saw it on their TV screens they started to call Cilla a liar and say that Elvis would never do such a thing, she recanted the lie, as the lie no longer served her and she wanted Elvis's fans to like her and go to Graceland to make her rich. Even the MMs have said Elvis wasn't capable of such a thing.

MYTH BUSTED.

CILLA MYTH THE MADONNA SYNDROME

This is possibly the next of the most destructive lies Cilla made. Cilla made a lot about this saying her reason for all her extra-marital cheating was because Elvis would not have sex with a woman who had had a child, sadly many believed her, including Mike Stone, who still believes it true in a recent interview, but we know it was just another Cilla lie. Joyce Bova wrote a whole book, she said was true, based on this lie. How do we know it was a lie, Cilla let it slip on an English day time TV show that the best sex they ever had was after Elvis's opening return night in Las Vegas, which was July 31, 1969, now as Lisa was born February 1st 1968, unless time is going backwards that was more than a year after Lisa was born. We also know Elvis had told just about everyone after Lisa was born he wanted loads more babies, and Elvis had overheard the conversation between Cilla and someone who worked at Graceland and Cilla saying 'not with me', that must of hurt Elvis terribly, but it did not stop him from trying to make his marriage work, even though he knew full well Cilla was cheating on him. Elvis has also had several girlfriends who were single parents, more evidence Cilla is a liar. How sad Joyce Bova did not check her facts before she wrote her book condemning Elvis, saying she had got pregnant but had an abortion because Elvis had told her he could not have sex with a woman who had a child. I am sure Elvis never said such

a thing or even thought it, is Joyce Bova a liar, many believe her against Elvis, how sad.
When Cilla lies the whole world hears it when she then recants her lie it would seem very few hear it, why is it that so-called fans want to believe the worst of him all the time.
MYTH BUSTED.

ELVIS NEVER TOOK HER ANYWHERE
One of Cillas myths is that Elvis never took anywhere, of course that is a lie, apart from taking her on holidays/vacations, he often took to engagements he attended and to shows and dinners in Las Vegas, as the photos prove. As well as the movies at the Memphian cinema and other places, the sad thing is how unhappy Elvis looks in the later photos when he knew  it was just a charade.
Elvis and Cilla at TJs night club New Years eve party in Memphis
MYTH BUSTED.

CILLA TAUGHT ELVIS TO RIDE HORSES

Now even if you remind them Elvis was riding horses long before he met Cilla they will say that because a horse ran away with him on the set of Flaming Star he was frightened of horses and it was Cilla who got him riding again, as with most Cilla myths/lies there is plenty of evidence to the contrary, in the movie Blue Hawaii, not only does Elvis look very happy riding the horse in the movie the horse looks pretty happy too, and if any animal knows you are afraid then they give you trouble and obviously this horse sensed no fear from Elvis. There are many photos of Elvis riding horses before and after he met Cilla. Elvis rode horses with June Juanico at a Dude Ranch in the late 50s, he

rode horses in many different movies too and Blue Hawaii was before Cilla moved into Graceland.

Above in Blue Hawaii in 1961. MYTH BUSTED

ELVIS WAS A GERMAPHOBE

Another one of Cillas myths is that Elvis was a germophobe, I have serious doubts if she actually knows what one is, she said he was one because he always had his own cup. Doesn't

everyone? and because he never took her out to dinner, which we know is also a lie because there are numerous photos proving he did take her out to dinner. How could he  possibly be a germophobe when he kissed all those women from the stage, something a germaphobe would never do.

There is even a photo of him eating snow.

MYTH BUSTED.

ELVIS TREATED CILLA AS A LIVING DOLL

Cilla always proclaims that Elvis always told her what to wear and how to have her hair, that her hair had to be jet black like his, what style she had to have and how her make-up had to be. This is not true, in fact it led to a falling out, I have read, between Patty Perry and Cilla, because Cilla kept on ordering Patty to make her hair bigger and bigger and Patty refused, partly because she knew Elvis preferred the

natural look.
  There are several photos Cilla with her hair blonde and without the trademark bouffant and eyeliner she often wore.

MYTH BUSTED

ELVIS TREATED CILLA AS A

ELVIS WOULD ONLY LET HER WEAR DRESSES

Cilla claims Elvis thought women should not wear trousers, so would not let Cilla wear them, but this is just another one of Cillas lies, again there are lots of photos of her wearing trousers.

MYTH BUSTED

CILLA LIVED IN A GILDED CAGE

This is again simply not true, Cilla could do and go anywhere she wanted, as with the photo of her blonde it is plain to see she is out somewhere, Cilla even went disco dancing to New York and took her friend Joanie Esposito and Jerry Schilling with her, who Elvis always suspected of being her lover after finding them alone in the kitchen one night, she was hardly locked in a cage. MYTH BUSTED.

PRISCILLA WAGNER BEAULIEU

In 1959 while Elvis was stationed in Germany Cilla already had a bit of a reputation it has been said for liking wild boys, and when she found out Elvis was there, she made it her mission to meet him. At the time Elvis had the image of being a wild boy even though he was not. It has been written that Cilla had intercourse with Curry Grant a DJ on the camp to get him to take her to meet Elvis, when the date was arranged, she got her mother to do her make-up and hair to look as much like Debra Paget as possible, Cilla even wore her mother's clothes to make herself look older. What parent does that for their 14yr old daughter so they can go to a rockstars house, who they do not even know till 3am, unless they have dollar signs in their eyes.

Unfortunately for Elvis he was immediately taken by her looks and her shy coyness, he said she looked like a china-doll, he was later to find out how much like one she was, she was cold and spoilt and used to getting her own way and had no heart, in his own words he tried to teach her how to love but she was cold and incapable of giving love.

In 'Child Bride' Cilla is quoted as saying she begged Elvis to consummate their relationship before he was shipped back to America, but he would not, he believed girls should be pure and virgins, he was soon to find once she joined him she was not so innocent. I have been told the reason Gene Smith suddenly disappeared from the scene was because Elvis found Cilla flirting with him, this would be one in a long line. I have been told every time Elvis was away doing a movie, she would find someone to spend time with. She thought Elvis didn't know but of course he did. Do not forget Elvis did not want to marry Cilla in his own words he was "railroaded", and others have said they found him crying about it and said he had to marry her, he couldn't get out of it.

He even had a private eye following her as he did when she and Jerry Schilling went to New York together, Elvis was already convinced they were doing it together after he found the pair in a compromising position late one night in the kitchen, with Cilla apparently only wearing a black see-through nightie, and this was before they were married, but the PI reported Cilla hooked up with a singer called Little Anthony while in New York.

She started dating her dance instructor Steven Peck, just three months after Lisa was born, who she even took to Elvis's 68 Special, can you imagine Elvis's embarrassment having her there with her lover on the back row, how he kept his cool I do not know. So when Elvis would not give her the divorce she wanted she upped the ante,

Elvis still trying to get her involved in what he liked asked her to go to a karate demonstration where she first saw Mike Stone, she later literally threw herself at Mike, according to him, so successful was Cilla, he left his pregnant wife for Cilla cause Cilla told him she would marry him once Elvis gave her the divorce, and to encourage Elvis to give her the divorce she paraded Mike all over Vegas while Elvis was playing there, embarrassing Elvis, now the whole world knew what was happening. When she left Elvis, she took Lisa and for two weeks Elvis never knew where they were, Elvis was going crazy thinking he would never see his daughter again. When Elvis still would not give her a divorce, she threatened she would use spousal rape as a reason for the divorce and ruin his career, so Elvis finally gave into her demands, later she ditched Mike Stone saying he didn't have enough ambition.

Elvis let her have everything she wanted with the one proviso that she was not allowed to use the Presley name for financial gain. Indeed, Parker wanted to TM the name, but Elvis did not think it necessary, it must be the only time I wish Elvis had taken Parker's advice. So Cilla was free to do whoever she wanted and she did, one of the men she went out with was Robert Kardashian, and he has said when Elvis would phone to speak to Lisa, Cilla would put the receiver on the pillow while they had sex so Elvis could hear, hoping to drive him crazy, Kardashian said she told him that she would not remarry till Elvis was dead thinking she would inherit everything.

Now Cilla makes a big thing about Elvis asking her to remarry him before he died. He did, but not because he wanted Cilla because he wanted Lisa full time with him, because he knew Lisa was only happy with him, Cilla had never had a good relationship with Lisa, as a baby Cilla was never there, so Lisa did not know who Cilla was, when the 'family' photos were taken Lisa cried when Cilla tried to pick her up. Elvis even told Cilla it would be an open marriage as he knew Cilla could never be faithful, but she said 'No'. Elvis had asked her because by then he knew Ginger was not going to be his wife, he didn't even bother telling Ginger he wanted full custody of Lisa, so when Cilla declined Elvis said that he might as well marry Ginger then, just to see what Cilla would say, not because he had any intention of marrying Ginger, remember I said Cilla thought she would inherit everything. It actually says in Child Bride that she was happy Elvis had died, that is until she found out Elvis had written her out of his will because he hated her greed, but that did not stop Cilla she coerced Vernon to let her be part of the board who made the decisions about EPE, in reality she was a figure head and makes a lot of money from using the Presley name but the decisions are not just hers and never have been, Elvis already had lawyers there to take care of business.

As soon as Elvis had been buried, she went off to Europe with her latest boyfriend and sent poor Lisa, who had just lost the most important person in her life to summer camp, how heartless can a woman be. Elvis was hardly cold in the ground when she sued Graceland estate for the rest of the divorce settlement, which was her daughter estate, the fact she had stolen numerous items from the different houses Elvis owned had never crossed her greedy mind it was wrong.

She also threatened to sue Joe for his family movies which he gave her, I have also read right after Vernon's funeral she went skinny dipping with the Stanleys and had sex in the back of the car with David to get their family home movies, obviously there was something in the home movies she didn't want anyone to see. She also wrote her horrible book about Elvis and made it into a TVM again claiming Elvis had raped her.

Cilla was a horrible uncaring abusive mother to Lisa both emotionally and physically, Mike Edwards tells of her dragging Lisa by her hair and bashing her the disturbance was so loud the neighbours called the police and this was at Mike daughters home, so if she would treat Lisa like that in public, imagine how brutal she must have been to her in private, and we know she thought it was funny that Mike admitted to her that he lusted after Lisa and would go into her bedroom at night but instead of throwing Mike out she left Lisa with him, Mike was allowed by Cilla to sexually molest Lisa for three years, Lisa herself said so, while Cilla went away on business, where she also met and dated Richard Gere and Julio Iglesias when she was away. Near the end of their relationship Cilla aborted Mikes baby and a while after they had finished, she phoned him one day, Mike thought to try and get back with him, but no she phoned to tell him she had met Marco and was having his baby instead.

Let me also add that not only did Elvis not want to marry Cilla in the first place but not long after they married he asked her for an annulment and he asked her if she wanted an abortion because he did not think the baby was his, only when he saw Lisa did he know it was, now does that sound like a man madly in love with her, no it does not, he never wanted to marry her and never trusted her, Cilla herself said Elvis asked for the annulment and if she wanted an abortion.

The list of lies Cilla has told about Elvis would probably fill a book but these are the more memorable ones, she said Elvis had a complex about being with mothers and that's why she had to take lovers cause Elvis wouldn't have sex with her, which we know is untrue. In her Barbara Walters interview, she say, " sex is everything, don't you think", Cilla made a big thing about this and many people to this day still believe that lie, but Cilla let it slip live on British daytime TV, when they were talking about Elvis's return to Las Vegas in 1969 she said that night they had the best sex they had ever had, when the presenter asked her about the 'Madonna' syndrome', she simply said she had to have an excuse for all her infidelities, as if that made it ok to tell that lie and make out Elvis had some kind of mental problem.

According to Elvis's maid after Lisa was born Elvis said he wanted to have lots more babies, when the maid told this to Cilla, Cilla replied, well he is not having them with me, or words to that effect. Then there is the unforgivable lie that Elvis raped her, I have to say she has now recanted these lies, and Elvis did not rape her, sadly many do not hear her recanting her lies and still believe them. It is sad that she thinks she can say such awful things about Elvis, and we will forget them.

One of her funnier lies she said was Elvis was a germophobe which is hilarious considering all the women he kissed from the stage and glasses he drank out of, now either Cilla is so dim she does not understand what she is saying, which I do not think so, or the more likely explanation is she thinks we ELVIS'S fans are too dumb to know.

Cilla and Barry Siegal tried to embezzle over a 100 million dollars from Lisa several years ago but Marco Cilla's partner and father of her son, overheard Cilla collaborating on the phone with Siegel, Marco told Lisa who sued Cilla to get it back successfully with Marco testifying for Lisa. I believe this is why and when Lisa decided to remove both Cilla and Barry Siegel from her will, Lisa never spoke to Cilla again as far as I can tell. Since then, Cilla and Navarone her son have led a smear campaign against Marco, the only person who tried to help Lisa since Elvis died. They have tried to say that Marco covered up his past and they did not know Marco came from Brazil, yet it clearly states in the book "Child Bride", that Marco went to the U.S.A. on a student visa and married a student in order to get his green card, and that is why Cilla could not marry him and got pregnant so quick with Navarone to keep Marco, who was a writer, producer and director of TV series and movies, so Cilla got what she had always wanted, someone who could make her a star.

When Ben tragically died Lisa invited her estranged mother to the funeral, but Cilla snubbed her daughter in her hour of need, that is the sort of person Cilla is. At the Golden Globes ceremony, they seated Cilla next to Lisa, Lisa did not sit next to her mother by choice, Lisa was clearly unwell, but Cilla did not so much as glance her way, let alone get her help as any other mother would for their daughter.

Cilla did some horrible things to Lisa, she may not have actually stabbed her in the back, but I think she is definitely responsible for Lisa's death. Cilla gave Lisa a horrible life once Elvis had died. Cilla joined scientology knowing full well Elvis called them a cult and would not want Lisa involved with them, but Cilla thought scientology could help her become a star. Cilla also used scientology as a baby-sitting service for Lisa dropping her off there whenever she had enough of Lisa. Cilla also put Lisa in 'obedience therapy' at scientology as a schoolgirl.

Anyone with a heart could have understood what Lisa was going through after losing Elvis, the person Lisa has said of, "the only person who made her feel safe", but not Cilla she treated Lisa as someone she did not want, Cilla has said in interviews that she never wanted Lisa. I believe it is those early days that Lisa spent with Elvis that kept her sane after everything Cilla put her through.

Within days of Lisa dying Cilla made a power grab for her granddaughter's inheritance, saying that she had not been made aware that Lisa had removed her, Cilla, from the trusteeship/will, she also has said the signature is wrong and the name is spelt wrong, what kind of mother does that. Even Joel Weinshanker, as well as others, have all said everyone knew Lisa wanted Graceland to be left to her children, why would Cilla even think that Lisa would not remove her after Cilla had tried to embezzle all that money from her, of course she removed Cilla and Siegel, Cilla's co-conspirator from her will, he is not contesting it, only Cilla, as always she is driven by greed and not love.

Cilla did some horrible things to Elvis as well, she thinks we do not remember all the nasty things she did and said to Elvis, and sadly some fans do not, it is almost like they are under some kind of spell by Cilla, we should feel sorry for them, hopefully one day their eyes will be opened. Cilla will never be happy or content. I think she is a Dark Triad; I do not make these claims rashly I have a diploma in psychology and counselling.

https://psychcentral.com/lib/beware-of-the-dark-triad

"*Child Bride*" by Susanna Finsted,

"*Priscilla, Elvis and Me*" by Mike Edwards

CALIFORNIA HIGHWAY PATROL

NOTICE TO APPEAR L 636452

DATE	TIME	DAY OF WEEK
10 - 30 19 71	10:25 AM	SAT

NAME (FIRST, MIDDLE, LAST)
PRISCILLA ANN PRESLEY

RESIDENCE ADDRESS (ST. OR ROAD) / CITY / ZIP CODE
144 MONOVALE, BEVERLY HILLS, CA

BUSINESS ADDRESS / CITY / ZIP CODE
5764 HWY 51 SO., MEMPHIS TN

DRIVER'S LICENSE NO. / STATE / BIRTHDATE
N 652453 CAL 5-24-45

SEX	HAIR	EYES	HEIGHT	WEIGHT
F	BRN	BLU	5-2	110

VEHICLE LICENSE NO. / STATE
153 CKU CAL

YEAR OF VEH.	MAKE	BODY STYLE	COLOR
71	MBENZ	RdSTR	WHT

REGISTERED OWNER OR LESSEE
ELVIS A PRESLEY

RESIDENCE ADDRESS (ST. OR ROAD) / CITY / ZIP CODE
1174 N. HILLCREST BEV. HLS

VIOLATION(S)
22349 U.C. EXCEEDING
MAX SPEED LIMIT

notice Cilla is living in Monovale road, since 1971 and not with Elvis.

How could Cilla allow this to happen.

ANN-MARGRET

Ann-Margrets first real taste of stardom came when she made the movie "Bye Bye Birdie", she took full advantage of her looks and feminine wiles to get George Sidney infatuated with her, making her a star in "Bye Bye Birdie", she was determined to climb the ladder of success anyway she could, and it worked, George only had eyes for her on set. George Sidney and Ann-Marget raised eyebrows canoodling onset on 1963's "Bye Bye Birdie". Their co-star Dick Van Dyke described one moment when he and Janet Leigh walked on to a sound stage to find Ann-Margret sitting on Sidney's lap. Both apparently looked at each other and said, "Uh-oh". It apparently infuriated leading lady Janet Leigh, who was a major star after the 1960 Hitchcock thriller Psycho, so much that she slapped George Sidney. "Janet Leigh was also furious to discover a new title song had been filmed in secret showcasing Ann-Margret. The film "Bye Bye Birdie" catapulted Ann-Margret to superstardom and George Sidney's infatuation was clear from the way he expanded her character's role.

George Sidney made sure Ann-Margret was given the lead in Viva Las Vegas he was infatuated with her, and her flirting continued, securing more scenes than she was supposed to get, favourable close-ups and extended musical sequences. He even famously managed to squeeze her into the final scene, stealing Elvis' thunder.

George Sidney said 'We made this picture, no problem. The only problem was Elvis didn't want the girl Ann-Margret to have any close-ups. He wanted all the close-ups. And he didn't want her to have any numbers. Well, I said, "No... I'm directing the picture. I'll do it my way." "This extended to the famous split-screen final scene where Elvis comes out singing while Ann-Margret dances and poses. They were clearly shot separately, and it was reported that Elvis had not wanted to share the limelight so Sidney secretly filmed Ann-Margret and then inserted her. This led to major confrontations with Colonel Parker and even Elvis himself. When the film was released in New York George Sidney didn't even give Elvis top billing, and Parker wanted to sue. Ann-Margret like so many others used Elvis and George Sidney to get her foot up the ladder to success.

Elvis was totally beguiled by Ann Margret she was like no other woman he had ever come into contact with, her zeal, confidence and continuous flirting with Elvis paid off, Elvis was totally taken with her, she has admitted how shy Elvis was when they first met, and she used the dance sequences to pursue him, knowing she could emulate his moves, Elvis felt a bond between them. Elvis was totally honest with Ann Margret from the very beginning of their relationship about Cilla, he told her anything that was between them had to remain strictly private or it could get him in a lot of trouble, (we all know Cillas step-father had warned Elvis one wrong move and he would sue him under the Mann Act and ruin his career and Elvis might even do jail time), so it was essential that no one found out he had been seeing her outside of the studio. Elvis being his usual generous self, bought her a round pink bed, but instead of keeping this strictly private as he had asked her to, she told her publicist, now she swears it was not her who told a London newspaper that they were engaged and Elvis had bought her a round bed, but someone did, either way it had broken a strict rule and Elvis's faith in her was shattered, but he forgave her as was his way and they continued to see each other. The announcement although quickly denied put a great strain on the already strained relationship Elvis had with Cilla and her stepfather.

A lot of people think their romance was the romance of the century, but it was not, Ann Margret was always looking for her next rung up the ladder to success, so much so while still seeing Elvis she went out for dinner with Roger Smith, Elvis was not happy, not happy at all. I have to say this, if you love someone, really love someone and they are tangled up in a relationship they do not want, and you know they love you, as I am sure Elvis did love Ann Margret, you wait for them, you do not jump for the next available man who comes along, which is exactly what Ann Margret did. (Now I know some will not believe me, but it is in black and white in the MMs book, now I know they lied a lot in that book, but all the MMs liked Ann Margret because, well, basically she flirted with them as well and treated them as equals and not at all as Elvis's watchers so seek out pge284, in fact there is a whole chapter devoted to her.)

Ann Margret has said in many interviews she knew she was going to marry Roger by their third date, now that does not say very much of her supposed love for Elvis. In fact, she married Roger just one week after Elvis married Cilla, as I have said before she must have known the marriage between Elvis and Cilla would not last because what Elvis had told her about Cilla, so why did she not wait for Elvis if she truly loved him, the simple answer is this, Elvis loved Ann Margret but she did not love Elvis, not real cannot live without you love, she loved the fact she got attention and she loved the fact that when Elvis came to one of her shows and went backstage to see her, her ticket sales went up. In the 70s once Cilla moved out it has been said Elvis visited Ann Margret often in her Vegas dressing room, and apparently she would take him into another adjacent room so they could be private together and Elvis got down on his knees and begged her to leave Roger to be with him, now she never did, but what decent married woman would even take a former lover into a room by herself knowing how infatuated Elvis was with her, whenever she opened in Vegas Elvis would send her flowers, now to me if she had a scrap of decency or any love for either Elvis or Roger she should have told Elvis not to visit her and not to send her flowers that she was happily married and did not want to make her husband jealous, but she did not, she led Elvis round by the nose like a love-sick puppy dog, giving him just enough hope to keep him going back to her.

When Ann Margret was encouraging Elvis in his desperation begging her to leave Roger on his knees, just so her ego would feel stroked, this is what she said in an interview in 1972, to me, this shows just how little she thought of Elvis and she had never even contemplated wanting Elvis as her husband, to me this is a real slap in the face for Elvis. "Now in Roger I've found all the men I need rolled into one — a father, a friend, a lover, a manager, a businessman," she told writer Rex Reed in 1972. "It's perfect for me. I couldn't exist without a strong man."

So, she was never interested in Elvis as someone she would marry only as someone to feed her large ego, Roger got her because he gave up his career to manage her. That is not love for Elvis that is love for her own ego. In another Ann Margret interview, she said she got along with Elvis because she loved her parents and Elvis loved his mother, totally dismissing

Vernon altogether, who was not only the closet to Elvis a father and son could be but was Elvis's rock and best friend, to me that is a terrible slur on Vernon. Ann Margret has also made it quite clear in interviews that Roger was the love of her life, not Elvis.

One of the things I cannot forgive her for is in all the interviews she has done, and there have been quite a few, when she is asked about Elvis in the 70s and his ill health and they ask her about him taking drugs never once has she stood up for Elvis and said 'the only drugs he took were prescribed medicines for his various health issue', NOT ONCE, no instead she sidesteps the issue and talks about something else making it look like she has something to hide. Maybe she is frightened they would bring up her own addictions after her fall that Roger helped her get over, but even if that is the case it does NOT excuse her from not standing up for Elvis, when you truly love someone, you stand up for them, you do not sidestep the issue making it look like you are hiding something.

Yes, Elvis loved Ann Margret, she loved herself and the fact that being associated with Elvis could get her the limelight like so many others we know. Had she really cared about Elvis she would have waited a few years for him and been there to help him, not lead him around like she did and make his depression worse in my opinion.

https://www.express.co.uk/entertainment/music/1432310/Elvis-Viva-Las-Vegas-Ann-Margret-love-affair-director-George-Sidney

https://www.closerweekly.com/posts/who-is-ann-margrets-late-husband-get-to-know-roger-smith/?fbclid=IwAR3u2d9flYN0goEZsKrocH04Vs88fhJX_uywDKayDKHNrV_171klZpMFt0g

https://www.closerweekly.com/posts/inside-ann-margret-and-roger-smiths-50-year-love-story/?fbclid=IwAR3rt4If-XLCZry-jPoR8_RCht9AbQt-dYjBCHz36f7yjfA0ghxk57EJ6L4

https://www.express.co.uk/entertainment/films/1430292/Ann-Margret-first-meeting-Elvis-Presley-Viva-Las-Vegas?fbclid=IwAR1HZl57JiBuMHe4zvvo6IgftXZ7gZFw2mboay8r_U3f6sJzdSJzBOroO4

https://www.latimes.com/local/obituaries/la-me-roger-smith20170605story.html?fbclid=IwAR0PPEIgltyNtoGWwvS0WRblweQk4JceNjJ10L0xhxUHVzCRBIQP6KsOZF0

Ann-Margret and Roger getting married just days after Elvis did to Cilla, had Ann-Margret had loved Elvis I think she would have waited, but her career was what was important to her, and Roger, not Elvis.

JOYCE BOVA

Joyce Bova wrote a book based on the claim
that she got pregnant with Elvis's baby, and had
it aborted because Elvis would not have sex with
a woman after she had had a baby, she then
claims she ended the relationship, which to me
makes no sense whatsoever, why have the
abortion so you can carry on having sex, but
instead end the relationship. Joyce Bova did
see Elvis a few times, but it was nothing like she
claims according to the MMs book. I think she
made the whole pregnancy think up and she is
bit of a fantasist. She jumped on Cillas
'Madonna syndrome' bandwagon without
checking her facts before she wrote her book.
We know it is a lie because Cilla admitted to it
when she accidentally said on live TV the best
sex her and Elvis ever had was after his 1969
come back in Vegas over a year after Lisa was
born. Cilla admitted the whole 'Madonna
syndrome' was a ruse to explain away her
infidelities and cheating on Elvis. We also know
Elvis said he wanted many babies after Lisa was
born, 20, according to Nancy Rook a maid who
was there when Elvis said it, so obviously the
'Madonna syndrome' cannot be true, or he
would not have said he wanted more babies with
Cilla, so we can also be sure Elvis never said
this to Joyce either, we also know Elvis would
have only had sex with a woman who told him
she was on the pill, like Linda T had. We also

know that Elvis had affairs with women both before Cilla and after who were single mothers.

This brings us to Barbara Leigh a single mother who Elvis had an affair with after Cilla left him, Bova said in her book that she was there when Elvis had to have an emergency procedure on his eye due to glaucoma, when a surgeon had to put a needle straight into Elvis's eye to relieve the pressure to save the eye, but in Dr Nicks book he says it was Barbara Leigh who was there next to Elvis, now I am sure Dr Nick would know the difference between a famous actress Barbara Leigh and Joyce Bova.

On the photo she has on the cover of her book Elvis wears a blue scarf over his shirt, this was when he was doing the Tribe of Dan and the colour of the scarf denotes how far along, he was, but she never mentions this in her book and it was a big thing to Elvis, surely, he would have mentioned something to her about it.

As I recall in her book, she makes it seem that Elvis flew to Washington D.C. to see her and seeing Nixon was an afterthought. The fact is that Elvis had written a letter on the plane about his fears and how he wanted to help the President, if President Nixon was the after-thought why would he have written the letter on the plane, he would have waited till after he had seen Joyce as she seems to infer. Elvis went to

Washington to see Nixon, he was on a mission to become a DEA agent and rid America of illegal drugs, it was Joyce who was the afterthought, if indeed he ever actually dated her at all, the only proof she has is a few photos of her with Elvis at Vegas. So please don't believe everything you read especially the sensationalised stories.

LINDA THOMPSON

LINDA ALWAYS MAKES OUT THAT SHE SAVED ELVIS'S LIFE BUT SHE WAS THE ONE WHO ALMOST KILLED HIM.
Linda gave him his sleeping meds and a bowl of chicken noodle soup in bed and walked away to her bathroom on the other side of the house to prim and preen herself, if she had had one thought for Elvis, she would have stayed till he got groggy took the soup away and laid him down, then gone to her bathroom.

When I first heard she had written a book, alarm bells started to ring, and they carried on when I read it and she was saying some very unkind things about Elvis and things that really did not need to be told. As he always did, he fell head of heels with her almost straight away and for the first year it seemed like maybe he had found someone who cared for him, but she got bored with the lifestyle and started going away for the weekends, Elvis had his suspicions especially after his experiences with Cilla, but he bent over backwards for her, even let her completely redecorate his home, while he was not there, so all the red is down to her, I have heard people say some unkind things about the way it was decorated, I have seen it described as a French bordello, but never as far as I know has Linda defended Elvis saying it was her who did the decorations and Elvis was not even there, no she lets Elvis's name take the stick for it. She did something unforgivable as far as Elvis was concerned as well, she took photographs of everywhere not just downstairs but his bedroom and bathroom she even let her friend sleep in his bed when he was away, he was furious about it.

As their relationship waned, he started looking for someone else, by now she was seeing David Briggs she says she did not start the relationship with him till after she finished with Elvis her best friend back then says different, Elvis wanted to finish with Linda when he found Sheila Ryan.

This is what her friend Stella Patchouli told me. It is in her book TEARS OF A SHADOW which is out of print but hopefully it is to be reissued shortly.
"People around him were there for one thing: MONEY AND FAME. They did not care about

him. I swear to God I cried when I realized these ppl, Linda, Joe, Jerry, everybody - cried 1 week, and then - they went on trying to find another sucker to mooch on. Linda would sit for hours on the phone, calling celebrity agents, introducing herself and asking to meet Joe Namath or Burt Reynolds...They'd reject. I'd take her to private clubs where Ringo Star and Ron Wood and Ryan O'Neil...and she'd walk up to them and say, "Hello, I'm Elvis' girlfriend of five years, Linda Thompson".... And my jaw would drop...She had a plan. I guess that's how you get rich. Note that Linda had her parents' support, so did Priscilla. Elvis seemed to be afraid of these PARENTS PEOPLE." Linda said when Elvis met Sheila Ryan, he wanted Linda out. "My mom and Dad got dressed up and went to see Elvis, threatening him that if he didn't buy me a house, they'd go to tabloid and TV and media and shame him and tell them everything about him. That's when Elvis bought her a house!!! Can you believe it?!!! Linda is very smart and greedy and stingy. Every man she caught; she used them to the max.' according to Stella.

Linda also ran up a huge credit card bill and Vernon had to tell her to give it back, I have heard she ran up as much as a 75-thousand-dollar debt on it, Elvis also had to pay for her apartment in LA as well even after he finally finished with her when he met Ginger. In Linda's book she claims she did not give the Wests permission to use a story about Elvis and her in their book, but her friend says otherwise, they asked her, and she said yes.

Also, in her book Linda makes a big thing about saving Elvis's life, but look at it this way, Linda had given Elvis sleeping pills many times, so she knew how quickly they worked on him. On this particular day she gives him his sleeping pill when he is in bed and then while he is sitting up in bed after the sleeping pill she gives him a bowl of chicken noodle soup, then she goes to her bathroom on the other side of the house and gets herself ready for bed, about twenty minutes later she goes back, Elvis has fallen asleep with his face in the soup, so how many brain cells did she engage when she left him, she might have got him out of the soup and cleared his throat but if she had been doing what she was paid very handsomely to do she would have stayed till he had fallen asleep not left him eating soup.

In her book she says he would ask her to make him his peanut butter and banana sandwich and she would say shall I get the cook to do it and he would say no I want you to do it with love, and he would watch her from the top of the stairs to see if she did, what she obviously missed out and so obviously did not understand is how important it was to Elvis that she do it for him because it showed she loved him, but she just did not get it, and Elvis had every right to be suspicious because often when he asked someone to do something for him they would then go and ask someone else, so he knew they did not want to do it for him. When you really love someone, you enjoy doing things for them which is what he was looking for, but sadly most of those around him were to self-serving, Linda, Cilla and Ginger included they did not seem to understand why he would ask.

Linda also seems to say in her book that when she did not go with Elvis on tours, she would be at Graceland which is not true, this is after he wanted to finish with her, because Elvis took the other girlfriends he had to Graceland, so Linda could not have possibly been there. Now she claims at every chance she gets that she was at every concert on tour or at Las Vegas, we know she is lying because Elvis met Sheila Ryan in Las Vegas and there are many photos to show they were often together at Las Vegas and other places, had Sheila accepted Elvis's request for her to move into Graceland Linda would have found her bags packed on the doorstep, also other girlfriends went on tour with Elvis and stayed at Graceland with him in the time period that Linda was still around like Diane Goodman and Mindi Miller.

Linda has said in the past that Elvis became impotent also a lie, Sheila goes into details about their intimacy and how good Elvis was and other girlfriends after Sheila have also said he had no problem in that department, the fact is

Linda turned him off, while she was with Elvis she was supposed to be taking the contraceptive pill, but Elvis found out she had stopped in order to pregnant, Elvis was rightly furious, he had been trapped in to marrying Cilla he didn't want it to happen again. Linda says after their first year they rarely had sex if ever, seriously after doing that why would he trust her again, what these women don't seem to realise is Elvis had to be in love with someone, and after that stunt he was no longer in love with Linda, so he found someone else, Shelia, Elvis wanted to move Sheila into Graceland but Linda would not budge, even when Elvis bought her a house, the 'perks' were too good as she said in a newspaper interview, and as we all know Elvis hated conflict, so she got to stay, especially as she had her parents threaten Elvis with going to a gutter rag, I have been told.

As a last insult she turned up to Elvis's funeral looking totally inappropriate in that dress, she could at least have worn something to cover her shoulders. What always bothered me about one of her stories was her lying about Lisa phoning her, she did not, her brother Sam was there looking after Lisa and he dialled his sister then gave the phone to Lisa, she tries to make out they were so close, yet after the funeral did she even see Lisa again, I cannot find one photo of an adult Lisa with Linda, just when Lisa needed her most, she wasn't there she was looking after herself finding her next victim.

Elvis wanted a stay-at-home wife to mother him and have his babies, someone equal with his own intellectual abilities who was interested in and understood all the alternative things he was interested in, someone who did not want any of his fame or limelight but happy to stay in the background, someone who would make him feel whole and not inferior. Sadly, this was not Linda, she was more interested in making a career for herself and wanted to be in the limelight, and I have been told Linda's only other concern is money, which we could see when she would not give Elvis's credit card back after he died but waited till she had maxed it out. I have been told when a friend of hers went to stay with her she was furious when the 'friend' helped themselves to a muffin without asking her permission, that is how selfish she was.

There is the story about the cross she 'bought' for Elvis for his birthday, he asked her how much it had cost him, she replied it could have cost him a lot more, or words to that effect, the point being, the fact she was spending Elvis's own money on him annoyed him, he would have much preferred something small she had bought with her own money, or better still something she had made for him and put love into.

When Elvis was with her he went from looking great to being in the deepest depression of his life cause he could not get rid of her, she was like an albatross around his neck, and I am sure you have seen the horrible pic of her looking like miss snooty and Elvis just about hanging on, that was her doing, by mid-76, he was so depressed he could not see a way out of it, fortunately he decided to move forward and made plans for his and Lisa's future, plans that did not include her.

What I do not understand is her continued obsession with making headlines through Elvis when she herself is a songwriter of some note, but this does not seem to matter to her. When she got married to Bruce Jenner, not only did they get married in Hawaii, Elvis's favourite place but they had an Elvis song 'The Hawaiian Wedding Song' playing for maximum exposure and sure enough it was in all the papers. I guess had she had one of her own tunes in a Las Vegas chapel it wouldn't have got so many headlines, and still she tries to be famous through Elvis doing Elvis conventions, with things like a mock-up of Elvis's bedroom and you can pay to lie on it with her, how low will someone go for a bit of money and publicity.

At the beginning of 2022, she had one of her unkind stories about Elvis on her Instagram account, everyone was else was saying how wonderful she looked, I told her I did not think it necessary to degrade Elvis with her story after all the things he had done for her, she blocked me, she only wants people around her who will suck up to her basically.

She is still making money off of Elvis's fans and telling lies about him, I guess she knows without her connection to Elvis she would still be nothing. According to google she is worth $25 million, so is it the limelight or the money she is still doing it for.

Linda also lies a lot to make herself look good and Elvis look bad as she did on her Instagram account, telling a lie saying Elvis was a desperate druggie who stole pills from a dentist surgery, apart from it being a total lie, anyone who thought about it would realise that Elvis if he needed pain meds or any other kind would never have to steal them he would just ask and he would be given, and what sort of dentist would have an open jar of meds sat there in his office, so that anyone could help themselves, they would be in a cupboard or under lock and key, or the receptionist would be watching all the time, it just does not make any sense, but her fans lap it up and never think to use their own common sense.

How can anyone believe she actually loved Elvis is beyond me and the fact that Elvis did not show her the door like most men would have, shows the hold she had over him, and why she was hardly on any of his tours or at Las Vegas with him no matter how much she says she was the photos of Elvis with others proves it, why would he want someone with him who made him do this, these are her words as quoted in a magazine:- "Being a bit of a germaphobe, when I went back to his dressing room after his show, I always made him brush his teeth, gargle, and sanitize his lips before I'd give him a kiss." Thompson acknowledged there were drawbacks to Elvis' career, but they didn't outweigh the perks.

She has also claimed that after Elvis's funeral, Vernon went to see her and got down on his knees and said if she had still been looking after Elvis he would not be dead, and thanked her for all the years she did look after Elvis. I sometimes wonder if her fans and they are supposedly Elvis fans ever engage their own brains, firstly her friend back then told me she went straight back to Los Angeles after the funeral, secondly Vernon was an ill man at 61 having had several heart-attacks already, so I doubt he would go and visit her and get down on his knees to her, especially from his comment about her in the Good Housekeeping interview, saying Elvis felt her love was choking him, and thirdly, Vernon was always convinced Elvis had been murdered so why would he say, if she had been looking after Elvis he would still be alive. If only these fans would read between the lines and realise virtually every story she tells makes her look like an angel and everyone else mad, bad, or sad.

Linda is also a marriage wrecker, she tried to wreck David Briggs marriage when she was cheating on Elvis with him, but he wouldn't leave his wife and kids, then there was David Foster, he left his wife for Linda, it shows what her moral compass is if she has one, she always puts herself first. It is so sad that supposed Elvis fans believe all her lies when there is so much evidence that she is lying, and so sad that a woman of her age does lie to get into the limelight to sell her book, why do these fans not realise she is taking advantage of them and laughing at them behind their backs. I often wonder if she realises the damage, she is doing to her soul with all this lying. Elvis is watching from spirit; he knows the truth.

GINGER ALDEN

Elvis met Ginger on the 19th of November 1976, George Klein took her sister to meet Elvis and Ginger tagged along and it was Ginger who caught Elvis's eye, tall with long dark hair and a former beauty queen, within three weeks of meeting her Elvis had already given Ginger a car. Elvis always fell hard and fast and was soon asking Ginger to move in, but she refused, so Elvis asked her to marry him and gave her a ring, now we know he gave her the ring in January on the 26th cause others have corroborated it, but we do not know for definite if

Elvis had asked her to marry him, but I suspect he did, he was very unhappy before he met Ginger and he wanted desperately to get married because not only did he want more children but he thought it would make it easier for him to get full custody of Lisa, which is all he cared about then, and Lisa gave him a reason to live. About the ring, Ginger said she hardly ever wore it and would leave it at Graceland in her book, now if I had been given a ring by Elvis it would have been as if it were glued to my finger, it would have never come off.

Elvis's favourite cousin, Bobbie Jane Ayers Wrenn, had committed suicide just before New Year's eve but they did not tell Elvis till after his New Year's eve show, because they knew how devastated Elvis would be, he cancelled the New Year's eve party and went straight home with Lisa and Ginger, now the very curious thing is when I asked Ginger about Lisa and about Elvis's cousin she had no idea about it, the excuse she gave about Elvis's cousin was that her grandfather had also just died and Elvis didn't want to upset her, but he did not go to the New Year's eve party as usual he went straight home with Lisa and presumably Ginger, how could she not notice Elvis was so upset, she was supposedly in love with him and when you are young and in love you notice every single thing about the person, unless you are so self-obsessed the only person you are interested in is yourself. I do not always believe what the

MMs said but every single one of them, Dr Nick, and anyone else who knew Elvis nearly all said the same thing, she did not love Elvis and she was only there for what she could get, and she got plenty.

When her grandfather died Elvis took her and her family there in his jet for the funeral, it is the photo she used on the front cover of her book about her and Elvis, and you can see at this point Elvis is still in love with her. Elvis was a very tactile person, and you can tell when he has gone off someone because there is no holding hands anymore or putting his arm around them.

By March of 77 the glow had gone, not only wouldn't Ginger move in with Elvis but Ginger always wanted to be with her family or her friends or be going out with them, it would seem anywhere except with Elvis. To begin with Elvis thought she was just shy and that was why she wasn't mixing with his friends, but from reading her book I think the truth is more that she felt she was above them, and in her book to me it seemed she felt the same about Elvis, she talked down to him like he was a child or something nasty she had stood in, and it seemed the only way to get her to be with Elvis was if he was buying her something, or her family something.

Elvis took her and her family and all his hangers on to Hawaii in the March it was according to Ginger some thirty people he paid for, and she seemed quite annoyed in her book that Elvis had paid for so many, but also in her book she wrote about the way she talked to Elvis and was even proud of herself for doing so. In Hawaii she said she told him off for drinking too much Papaya fruit juice, (which in actuality is supposed to be good for digestive issues) not alcohol, or soda, or something else bad for you, no she told him off for drinking too much fruit juice, and she didn't do it in a manner that Elvis would have accepted like telling him all that acid might give you a bad stomach or all the natural sugar in fruit juice is bad for your diabetes, no, she just flat out told him he could not have any more, like he was a child, not a man with his own mind. At a different time in her book, she says she told him off for eating too much ice-cream and she was so nasty to him about it he threw it at the wall, and she proudly says in her book, something like, well at least he couldn't eat it then, I seriously do not know how he tolerated her for so long. One of the saddest things for me to read was that she said Elvis used to ask her if she loved him, imagine he was so desperate for her love he had to ask her to say it, to me it shows how self-absorbed she was, how could she make him practically beg like that, I would be ashamed to admit doing something like that to any human, but the man you are supposed to love, it is horrible.

But back to Hawaii, Hawaii was a test, and she was too self-absorbed to notice this. Elvis wanted her to spend the holiday with him obviously, but she didn't, most of the time she was with her family on the beach or shopping and Elvis was left alone in his room, his heart-breaking, yes, he is smiling in the photos from the holiday he was a good actor, notice the day of the photos where he is playing ball he is not in the direct sun, he couldn't be because of his glaucoma, now Ginger must have known about his glaucoma, and she must have known he couldn't go out in the bright sunshine with her. Also notice the photos of them on the beach he is flirting with or being flirted to by Joes girlfriend Shirley, this was always a big no between Elvis and the guys so much so one of them wrote one time with Cilla none of them would help her get off a boat cause it would mean touching her hand and none of them touched any of the others girls or wives, but here we see Elvis with Shirley all over him, now Elvis probably let it happen to make Ginger jealous but I feel it put a nail in his coffin as far as Joe was concerned. Elvis also got cosy with Gingers sisters too, but it didn't matter to Ginger because she wasn't there for Elvis, she was there for herself.

When you read her book, it is like a shopping list of fur coats and cars that he gave not just to her but to her whole family, for Elvis it was the only way he got to see her was when he had bought her or her family something and the only way it appeared she would go on tour with him was if her family came along too. Now I know for a fact Elvis had no intentions of marrying her, because when I asked her about Elvis getting full custody of Lisa, she knew nothing about it, now if Elvis was going to marry her and expect her to be Lisa's new mamma then he would have done more than mention it to her. All those who knew him said Elvis had Alicia Kerwin waiting in Portland, who George had introduced to Elvis in the April after the Hawaii fiasco, which he had cut short not because of sand in his eye, but because he was so upset with Gingers behaviour towards him. I know in June of 77 he was trying again to find her replacement, sadly Elvis could not bear to be alone, though for all intense purposes he was alone anyway, cause Ginger was hardly ever there. I know he had contacted two different women he had known in the past wanting and needing a relationship with one of them at least and for different reasons it never happened, one was because of Joe and the other was down to circumstances. So, no way was Elvis going to marry Ginger no matter what she says. If you have ever been on her page on Facebook you will see how she plays the martyr all the time, or did, she through me off for asking questions she could not answer, like the one about Lisa, or how could you not know about the Wests and Heblers book when it was all Elvis thought about and talked about that year, he was totally eaten up by it, but she once again was oblivious to it, on her page she claims everyone is a liar and is out to get her, she always seems to play the victim.

If Elvis had intended to marry her, he would not have made Ginger a witness of his will as witnesses cannot be beneficiaries, I think he made her and Charlie witnesses because he knew neither of them would tell Cilla that she was no longer going to get anything or that everyone else had also been removed from the will. Even Elvis's father did not think they were going to get married, in his interview after Elvis's death with the Good Housekeeping magazine he said, "I never got to know Ginger Alden well. She's not much of a talker, but a while back Elvis told me he'd fallen in love with her. 'This is the love I've been searching for', he said. 'I want more children, a son. And I want Ginger to be my children's mother'. After that, Ginger and Elvis came over to show me her engagement ring. That was one of the few times I'd ever seen her smiling. I assumed they were going to get married, but nothing happened and whenever I tried to talk to Elvis about Ginger, he'd seem upset. Finally, just a day or so before he died, I told him, 'I keep hearing and reading that you're going to announce your engagement. Is that right? When are you going to get married?' 'Only God knows', Elvis said. I got a feeling then that maybe he was changing his mind about marriage." For Vernon to say this it is huge as he never talks badly about anyone.

In Gingers book she said she told Elvis that she was not a virgin and had had other boyfriends before him, in fact Elvis suspected she was still seeing one of them and had a PI on her like he had done with others before. Now she also says in her book she was on the pill, but her reason for not waking the day Elvis died was that she had taken meds because she had bad period pains, now I can remember doctors giving girls the pill to stop them from having bad period pains and heavy periods, so I find that puzzling, her period was also the reason she said she didn't want to go on tour with Elvis. She says after waking she went to her bathroom to shower because she was flooding, why walk all the way to her bathroom on the other side of the house when Elvis's bathroom was right there, adjacent to the bedroom and she had to walk past it and she had noticed the door ajar, so why did she not use that bathroom. If the door was ajar, then she had no reason to think anyone was in it. When I used to wake up flooding I went to the nearest place, I would not have risked dripping blood all along the corridor. So Ginger says after she washed she phoned her friend and mother, her mother reminded her that Elvis had arranged for her brother to meet them on the tour, so Ginger decided she would go look for Elvis and tell him she would go after all, now if this is true it is a slap in the face for Elvis, because she was only going to go on tour to see her brother not to be with Elvis, as it was

Elvis was dead when she found him. There has been speculation she wasn't even there that she had been out partying and had come back to get her things because Elvis had told her to be gone by the time he got back off tour. A reporter from the Enquirer swore he had talked to Ginger that day and she had asked him to come to Graceland later that day because she had a big story for him, I think if that is true, she was going to sell her story and let him take photos inside Graceland thinking Elvis would have been on tour by then. Although some are not as kind about it as me, some have suggested she knew Elvis was dead cause when she came in and went up the back staircase, she stepped over Elvis's body, and that is why she needed to shower to get the smell of the nightclub off her and the 'friend' was the enquirer guy and then she phoned her mother, and then pretended to find Elvis.

After Elvis died like some others, Gingers family tried to sue Elvis's estate, his daughters, because she said Elvis had promised to buy her mother a house, fortunately she lost. What she did do however was follow her modelling and acting career using her association with Elvis, she made a horrible film that was supposedly based on her story of being with Elvis, of course she denies knowing it was about her and Elvis. Ed Parker apparently got her the part and then disappeared. The movie was called 'Living legend the king of rock and roll' and was about a young girl married to the king of rock and roll and his downward spiral blah blah blah and she claims she did not know it was about Elvis, how dumb does she think we are. IMDB says 'The story revolved around Eli Caulfield, the King of Rock & Roll. On stage, he is supreme, in his private life, nothing goes right, and his health is jeopardized by the overuse of prescription medication. An obvious reflection of the life of Elvis Presley.' if everyone else could see it how come she could not.

Ginger got married and had a son called Hunter, and just after her book came out her husband died of a sudden unexpected heart attack on the anniversary of Elvis's death, he died on the 16th of August 2015, a bookie would never take odds like that, and Elvis said there was no such thing as coincidences. Someone who said Ginger was a cousin said her husband had committed suicide, of course Ginger will not admit to that, so we are left with the impossible odds that someone who was engaged to Ginger and later her husband both died on the same day. There are many stories of people finding Elvis unhappy, even crying cause Ginger had left him alone once again, sometimes in the middle of the night, he would fall asleep with her and wake to find her gone, over the time she knew him she broke his heart as much as any of them, when he needed someone the most who understood him and wanted to be with him. All I can say in summary is I think she was totally absorbed with her own importance and was a gold-digger, she did not love Elvis only his money like some others. In credit to her she has not as far as I am aware told any horrific lies about him like some have. What I am sure of is Elvis had no intention of marrying her, when he introduced her in the CBS special, he introduced her as his girlfriend and not his fiancée, he did not even ask her to show the ring like he had done with Sheila, and was actively looking for his next girlfriend and had been since the April, after the Hawaii fiasco, when George Kline introduced Elvis to Alicia Kerwin.

Family Bans Presley's Fiancee

By DAVID WRIGHT and GWEN YOUNT

Ginger Alden — Elvis Presley's live-in fiancee at the time of his death — has been banned from Graceland, his Memphis mansion. And she's not even allowed to visit his grave without permission.

"Ginger Alden is dead now as far as the family is concerned," declared Vester Presley, the rock idol's uncle. "We don't even recognize her as a human being."

"Ginger has been shunned so completely that even the public has greater access to Graceland than she does. Elvis admirers who want to visit his grave need simply line up at the mansion gate to be let in. Not Ginger.

She must get special permission from Presley's father, Vernon — either by calling him in advance or by going to the mansion gate and having a guard phone him from there.

Vester, who often guards the gate, told The ENQUIRER:

"She couldn't get in here on her own to save her life, she's barred from inside the house. She can go to the grave — by calling and asking. Any time she comes in this gate I've got to call Vernon and O.K. it.

"We've not interested in her. She took advantage of Elvis' name. Now she's even making some kind of movie about him."

Vester was referring to "The Living Legend," in which Ginger plays the girlfriend of a rock idol. It's fiction but obviously inspired by Elvis' life.

Sitting in the wooden hut by the gates of Graceland, Vester told The ENQUIRER:

"Ginger just wanted to come in here and take over. Yes, just don't do that kind of thing unless you're really married. She was

her there's good and bad scene to go about it. You can't go pushing the family around. You can't treat them like they're dogs.

"She was money and unbearable. She had it in her mind to take over the house.

"I guess she thought she was better than us. She thought she was somebody. She bossed the servants all the time.

"She had her clothes moved in, and got to bringing her family in and coaxing Elvis to buy stuff for them. She tried her influence with Elvis to get him to buy her family presents."

The Aldens are bitter about what has happened. Echoing the family's feelings, Walter Alden, Ginger's father, complained:

"If Elvis could only know how they treat her when she goes to the gate (of Graceland). Ginger would have liked to keep up a close relationship with the Presleys. Elvis would have wanted it that way."

"Ginger was only one of the girls Elvis was dating. He would have been a fool to marry a woman like that, with his money."

"She tried to take over the role of mistress of Graceland.

COMPLETELY SHUNNED, Ginger Alden can't even visit Elvis' grave without special permission.

MARRIAGE

One of the enduring untrue myths about Elvis is that he was a womanising man who never wanted to get married, although Parker and the film studies started this, his so-called friends and some of his relatives have perpetuated it since he has been dead, when is reality nothing could be further from the truth.

In the long interview he says when he left school and got a job to become an electrician, he was waiting for his then girlfriend to graduate from school so they could get married, so right away he wanted to settle down and get married. He was crazy about Debra Paget in his first movie and wanted to marry her. He wanted to marry Anita Wood before he went to Germany, but Parker would not let him saying it would ruin his career. When he came out of the army, he made the film 'Blue Hawaii' with Joan Blackman, she says they had rooms next to each other while filming and virtually lived together and he asked her to marry him, so intent was he that when he made 'Kid Galahad', he requested her as his lead co-star so they could rekindle their relationship, but she still refused.

Then there was Ann-Margaret, had the media not got involved and had she not told anyone he had bought her a bed and it said in the newspaper he had asked her to marry him, he might well of, but he felt betrayed because by now he had Cilla there Ann-Margret knew all about her and the fix Elvis was in, had she stayed silent and let Elvis sort out the mess with Cilla and her father first he could well have married her, had she wanted him.

Now we know had Cilla been faithful to Elvis he would have been faithful to her, but she never was, not before they were married or after. I have been told even before she had Lisa she was playing around, which is why Elvis did not believe the baby was his and had planned on getting a paternity test done until he saw Lisa, then he knew Lisa was his, but it shows he knew Cilla had not been faithful to him at all and she has admitted to having an affair with her dance instructor just after Lisa was born.

So, after Cilla Elvis's first big love was Linda, and although Elvis fell hot and fast as he always did, she started to push him about marriage and babies and stopped taking the contraceptive pill I am told, then she started going away for weekends it reminded Elvis of how he had been forced into marring Cilla and her unfaithfulness and the relationship crumbled. Then she showed a complete lack of respect for Elvis by photographing not just the downstairs after he had let her redecorate (he went to a motel while it was being done) but Linda photographed his bedroom without asking him and let her friend sleep in his bed, he was not happy with his privacy being violated.

When he met Sheila he tried to end it with Linda but she would not go, she enjoyed the perks too much, she actually got her father to go and threaten Elvis that he would take the story to one of the gutters mags, this is when Elvis bought Linda a house to get her out of Graceland, sadly Sheila who he really had fallen for did not wait and married James Caan, but I think Elvis would have married her if she had not been so quick to leave.

Then came Ginger and once again Elvis fell head over heels and asked her to marry him within a few months of going out with her, Elvis really wanted to be married no matter what others might say, sadly as time went on he realised it was not shyness like he thought to begin with, she really did think herself better than him and talked down to him like something stuck to the bottom of her shoe, like she says in her book, and Elvis realised she was not who he thought and he was not going to marry her no matter what she says. Elvis also had his suspicions about Ginger and David Stanley I have read and hired a PI to follow her on her jaunts to discos and bars. I asked Ginger about their plans for the future and Lisa, she had no idea what I was talking about so I said it plainly to her had Elvis talked to her about him getting full custody of Lisa and her being Lisa's new Mom, and she said 'No', so no way was Elvis about to marry her as he had not discussed his most important plan for the future, but all through his life he was looking for someone to be his wife and have his children, he really was the marrying kind, he just never found the right person. You can listen to Elvis talking about this and many other things in the interview link below.
https://www.youtube.com/watch?v=XtuWKqfUzU E&t=6s

CHAPTER THREE

Elvis's quote

"PEOPLE THINK YOU'RE CRAZY WHEN YOU TALK ABOUT THINGS, THEY DON'T UNDERSTAND"

WHAT ELVIS REALLY BELIEVED IN

Since Elvis was a small child, he knew he was different, whether it was his longing to have his dead brother with him that opened him up to so much I am not sure, what I do know is Elvis learnt from an early age to not let anyone know what he was thinking or doing. As a small child Elvis used to talk to his dead brother Jesse, but when his mother found out instead of letting it go and thinking it was Elvis's way of dealing with his grief, a grief that she had imposed on him. Gladys was the one who told him about Jesse and made him feel responsible for his death. Vernon said they were not identical, just as Lisa's twins are not. Gladys had put it in Elvis's head that he had done something bad to Jesse to make him die. Right near the front of Elvis's Uncle Vester's book, he says that Vernon and Gladys had been hit by another car on Gladys's side when she was pregnant and that is where Vernon got the money from to build their house. So personally, I think this is what ultimately killed Jesse, maybe a small tear in his placenta, not enough to kill him outright but enough so he did not develop to full term, for some reason and I can only guess it was Gladys who put the notion in Elvis's head Jesse had been starved and it was Elvis's fault. Larry mentions it in his book. Can you imagine a child of three years trying to sort out that kind of information in his head, it is amazing Elvis adapted so well, but alas when

Gladys found out Elvis had been talking to Jesse she washed his mouth out with soap and water and warned him never to do it again or he would be put in a mental institute, so Elvis learned to keep it a secret, but in spite of his mother he carried on talking to Jesses, becoming more and more spiritual and less religious.

This opened up a whole new metaphysical world for Elvis of alternative beliefs, June Juanice is quoted as saying this: - Elvis and June had been standing on a pier in Biloxi and as they were gazing up at the stars Elvis told June to relax and imagine floating in space between the moon and the stars. If she relaxed enough, he said to her she would be able to float right up there next to him. June asked Elvis how long he had been doing this. Elvis told her since he was a little boy. He said he had learned a long time ago not to tell anyone cause people think you are crazy when you talk about things they don't understand'. It was June who gave Elvis his first copy of "the Prophet". Elvis's beliefs and abilities grew greatly, he could astral travel, talk to the dead, he believed in reincarnation, that he was an old soul who had been born many times, Elvis was telepathic and telekinetic, there are many stories of him stopping the rain and moving the clouds. Elvis was also a great healer and cured one of his backing singers cancer, to which she gives testimony to on YouTube. He believed in numerology and astrology, reading auras, colour therapy and much more. Many have said Elvis had an aura about him so great you knew he was coming before he entered the room, his 'gate-people', the fans who lived their lives at the gates of his different houses have said you could 'feel' when he was home, cause he did not always come through the front, sometimes he would go in the back way but the just 'knew' when he had. So, in this chapter I want to explore all these things Elvis could do and what his inner beliefs were.

WHERE DO WE COME FROM?

Elvis believed in aliens and UFOs, there are several stories about him seeing UFOs in different places, in the sky over Graceland and in the desert, and Elvis was fascinated by Von Daniken's books on ancient aliens, 'Chariots of the Gods and read it as soon as he could. Most ancient civilisations all say we came from the stars, that the earth was seeded by aliens/gods from the stars, Australian Aborigines, ancient Egyptians, most of the native American tribes like the Hopi and many others, the people of Meso-America and South America, the Toltec, the Mayan, the Incas and many others, Also African tribes and ancient Europeans, like the ancient Britons and the Vikings, and some religions like Hindu believe we came from the stars. Most think we came from the area where Orion's Belt is, like the three great Pyramids show and most think it was from Sirius star system, and coincidentally (Elvis said there are no coincidences) Sirius radio plays mostly Elvis's songs. Remember Vernon saying there was a blue light in the sky when Elvis was born, is this to do with the Hopi blue star kachina legend.

https://www.booksfact.com/technology/ancient-technology/the-hopi-prophecies-and-a-blue-star-kachina.html

So, do we all come originally from Sirius, click on the link to find out more?

http://askingangels.com/articles/starseeds/sirians.php?fbclid=IwAR281nHtHYziRXSXpNGcHlMqij3vz1tPkJBnFIChX402L1f2csnZUqUUI0

Not long ago a signal was received from outer space, it came from two black holes merging and it was the tune from Elvis's song 'Can't Help Falling in Love' that Elvis finished most of his 70s shows with. Was he sending us a signal, is that possible, people who believe in an afterlife might think so, read about it on the link below.

https://www.science.org/content/article/gravitational-waves-reveal-unprecedented-collision-heavy-and-light-black-holes?fbclid=IwAR3k_AXV1CdNvDlPnJbpnfK1ILzZ4fWi1bNQ75_pqwW3kWgyc6uES_gUsc4

ELVIS WAS A SUPERHUMAN

Most people will scoff and say he was just a normal man with a good voice, some may say a few more nice things, but the fact is Elvis was far from normal, Elvis was/is a very old soul, so old he was in tune with the cosmos and as such had abilities most of us could only dream of, he was supernatural or superhuman as many have attested too. Elvis was telepathic, telekinetic, psychic, prophetic, he could control the weather and his aura/presence was so great you could feel him walk into a room as just about anyone who ever met him has said, the fans at the gates of Graceland and Hillcrest have said his presence was so great you could even feel when he was at home from the gates. Just think of how Elvis literally changed the world and now even over 45 years later he is still touching people's lives, there are not many people that have ever done that.

One of the greatest things he could do was heal, there are so many stories of him doing that, not only while he was alive but since he has died a book has been written about it called "Life Afterlife" by Raymond A Moody Jr., M.D. Even Charlie told a story about a little deaf girl in his book. But for me the most compelling evidence of his super abilities is the testimony of Sylvia Shemwell, one of Elvis's backing singers, ELVIS CURED HER CANCER. Elvis noticed she was not her usual happy self and asked what was wrong. She told him she had cancer and she had to see other doctors the next day, Elvis said he was not going to let anything bad happen to her and he stayed up all night with her, healing her. The next day when she saw the doctors who did more tests, they said they could not believe the cancer was gone. Please take a few minutes of your time and listen to her and how Elvis cured her cancer.

https://www.youtube.com/watch?v=M0HMXTP3vOs

TELEPATHY

Telepathy is like a two way street or like a two way radio, you have someone sending the thought or vision and someone on the other 'end' to receive it, I am sure most of us at some time in our life have known who was at the door or on the other end of a phone line before we answered it, that is telepathy, most probably do not even realise they are being telepathic. Elvis was very telepathic, Sheila Ryan said Elvis often knew exactly what she was about to say before she said it, and there are many more anecdotal stories of his telepathic abilities, most mothers have a telepathic connection with their children, we 'instinctively know' some would say when something is wrong, that is telepathy, so

here is a story of Elvis's telepathy and his
mother Gladys getting it.

In early March 1955 Elvis bought his first Pink
Cadillac. It was a pink and white 1954 Cadillac
and provided transportation for Elvis and the
Blue Moon Boys for about three months. The car
went up in smoke when a brake lining caught
fire, on the road between Hope and Texarkana,
Ark. June 5, 1955. You can see how bad it was
by the photo, and how easily if Elvis and his
girlfriend had not of got out in time they could
have died or been seriously injured.

After a show at Hope, AR. Coliseum in Fair
Park, Elvis sets off for Texarkana with a girl from
that town, while Scotty Moore and Bill Black ride
with other friends. About halfway to Texarkana,
in Fulton, Arkansas, Elvis' pink--and--white
Cadillac catches on fire and burns. Elvis' mother,
Gladys, will always recall how she was
awakened out of a sound sleep at home by the
feeling that something was wrong. Others recall
Elvis sitting by the side of the road, looking
desolate as he watched his dreams go up in
smoke. From Texarkana Scotty returns to
Memphis to get the new pink and white Ford
Crown Victoria that Elvis has recently purchased
for his parents, while Elvis and Bill fly on to
Texas.

As you can see by the state of the car, had Elvis and his girlfriend not got out in time they would have perished, what a horrible dream for Gladys to have with no way of getting it touch with Elvis to make sure he was ok.

WAS ELVIS A SHAMAN IN A PREVIOUS INCARNATION

A shaman, a medicine man, a spirit walker, a healer. I think he quite possibly was, after all, in this life he talked to the dead, healed people like with Sylvia Shemwell's of her cancer, and he loved to astral travel. To

me when I see him in his totem suit a shaman is exactly what I see. 'The term shamanism comes from the Manchu-Tungus word šaman. The noun is formed from the verb ša- 'to know'; thus, a shaman is literally **"one who knows"**. Shamans are the most notable of the multiple religious figures present in traditional Aboriginal religion. They function as '**healers, prophets, diviners.'** This sounds just like Elvis to me, people have often said that he knew things, what people were thinking before they did even, he had a natural ability to know what was going on with another person. Another site says, 'The Shaman is believed to have a spiritual connection with animals, supernatural creatures and all elements of nature.' We have all heard of Elvis's ability to control the weather, I am sure as I can be he had all attributes of a shaman, although maybe most of those he knew did not realise it, most of what Elvis did and enjoyed doing, like talking to spirit, astral travel and having out of body experiences, his connection to nature and animals is all shamanistic, sadly most of those around Elvis treated these qualities as a joke and did not understand this side of his personality, so he mostly kept it to himself though he did let a few in.

for more info on shamans please click on the links below: -

https://www.amnh.org/exhibitions/totems-to-turquoise/native-american-cosmology/transformation-and-shamanism

https://www.warpaths2peacepipes.com/native-american-culture/shaman.htm
https://druidry.org/resources/shamanism-in-the-celtic-world

THE MAYAN CALENDAR

The Mayan calendar jumpsuit was often wrongly called the Mexican Sundial. We know Elvis had an unquenchable thirst for knowledge of all sorts of things, a need to know about all the ancient civilisations, which included the Ancient Chinese, Egyptian, Native American, Mesoamerica and South American, which included the Mayans. Elvis first wore this suit in 1974 not only in 1977 as some think. He wore several suits in 1977 this was just one of them, he also wore, The Chief, Arabian, and Rainfall as well as the Mayan calendar.

Myrna Smith has said that Elvis read a lot of books on the Mayan civilisation, so he knew all about the Mayan calendar way back then, it only came into most people's lives around 2010 when it was supposed to have foretold the end of civilisation and the world in 2012, some of you might remember it, it was in the papers practically daily, but it did not foretell the end of the world, only the end of a cycle, and it just happened to be the last of the calendars they produced, so 2012 came and went and we are still here.

I truly believe that Elvis had a premonition to do with this calendar, whether a dream or vision quest or when he was meditating and he thought it had to do with his death. I think Elvis thought that he too was going to die in 2012, in 2012 Elvis would have been 77 years old, but sadly

Elvis read the vision wrong, instead of dying at the age of 77 he died in 1977.

REINCARNATION

Elvis firmly believed in reincarnation and believed he was a very old soul. I would like to share with you different incarnations I think he may of had, the names of these historical people came to me, I would like to think from Elvis, and I have researched them and found out that they bare many similarities in character to Elvis, and coincidently there are also names which seem to have followed him through many lives as well as you will see. Coincidences are something Elvis always said that there is no such thing as coincidences, and everything happens for a reason, or another quote I heard was the universe is far too busy to make coincidences happen for anyone. The last two incarnations are ones Elvis himself had told different people about, and then a story of a life I believe that we shared together.

I believe it is through Elvis's strong telepathic abilities that he and I have been able to connect to each other and with his help explore these reincarnations. Please try to keep an open mind while you are reading these, after all, if you believe in reincarnation, we all had to be someone in the past, and as I have no way of researching people who would be unknown to the public now, I have researched those I can, historical people.

ANCIENT EGYPT

Elvis had a strong affinity with ancient Egypt, he called Memphis his home, even though he was born in Tupelo, Memphis was the capital city of ancient Egypt when I believe Elvis ruled there, even the front of Graceland is symbolic of Egypt with its triangular porch, representing a pyramid and the pillars of ancient lands, also the lions, what today are called the sphinx's many believe were once lions crafted in the time of Leo. Elvis had lots of jumpsuits reminiscent of his past lives, the native American inspired ones, the Mayan and the dragon of China from those lives, but most prolific were his Egyptian inspired suits, he had a suit called Pharoh, two different suits called Arabian, the Egyptian, a white Egyptian bird and a blue one too and a Peacock one. Elvis seemed to find comfort in the memories of Egypt be them conscious or subconscious, it was a time when he was happy and he absorbed himself in many of their ancient teachings, such as reincarnation, an afterlife and their believe in sky people (aliens) conversing with the dead in fact virtually everything of the ancient middle eastern philosophies. He even had peacocks in his garden which symbolised eternal life, and he liked his women to wear eyeliner like they did back then, he even wore eyeliner and eyeshadow himself in the early days of his career as Elvis as he would have done in ancient Egypt. Elvis even had a pyramid ring and often wore an ankh, another symbol of eternal life.

Elvis's ankh blue stone

Elvis' Pyramid Ring.... The auction website said, "With the exception of the TCB ring, this may be the most exquisite ring Elvis owned

ANTIOCHUS I THEOS OF COMMAGENE

Who was Elvis in ancient Egypt? Antiochus I Theos of Commagene bears a striking resemblance to Elvis, especially when he was younger, in 1956 'Scientific America featured a front cover with a statue of Antiochus on it, it was the same year Elvis broke on to the world-wide music scene, is this just a coincidence, Elvis always said there was no such thing as coincidences, everything happened for a reason.

Antiochus is said to have been very generous, good looking and had a sweet singing voice, sounds just like Elvis to me. Others think Elvis could have been Ramesses II this is a description of Ramesses, Ramesses the Great's mummy shows that he stood over six feet in height with a strong, jutting jaw, thin nose, and thick lips. Ramesses also suffered from arthritis the same as Elvis, he was also very intelligent and learned the same as Elvis, of course we will never know who Elvis was in the past but what we do know is he believed in reincarnation, and he had a strong resemblance to certain people in the past, and in this life collected things around him that possibly reminded him of past lives like those in ancient Egypt.

https://www.youtube.com/watch?v=FMEPNCdL Zel&t=1s

APOLLO

I have not been told if Elvis thought he had been Apollo in a previous life or not, after all as a mythical figure a god of ancient Greece and Rome did he even exist, I do not know, but I do know Elvis had a statue of Apollo. When you read about Apollo you could very well

be reading about Elvis, Apollo has been recognized as a god of, healing and disease, archery(you could change that for Elvis love of guns, a modern form of archery so to speak), music, dance and the arts, sunlight, prophecy and knowledge, order and beauty, herds and flocks, and protection of the young, a perfect blend of physical superiority and moral virtue, in time,

Apollo evolved to become a multifaceted god adored all over Greece as the perfectly developed classical male nude, the *kouros*. Beardless and athletically built, he is often depicted with a laurel crown on his head and either a bow and arrow or a lyre and plectrum in his hands. The sacrificial tripod – representing his prophetic powers – was another common attribute of Apollo, to me all those things are Elvis, I do not know if Elvis did archery but he was an excellent marksman with a gun as he proved in the army, protection of the young as well is so Elvis, he loved children and whenever you see a photo of him talking to a child he always went down to their level he never towered over them and we all know the rest is everything that Elvis was. Apollo like Elvis also had a twin. Apollo also looks like Elvis or should that be the other way around.

https://en.wikipedia.org/wiki/Apollo

WAS ELVIS DAVID (BIBLICAL)

David was the youngest son of Jesse, David began his career as an aide at the court of Saul, Israel's first king. He so distinguished himself as a warrior against the Philistines that his resultant popularity aroused Saul's jealousy, and a plot was made to kill him. He fled into southern Judah and Philistia, on the coastal plain of Palestine, where, with great sagacity and foresight, he began to lay the foundations of his career. As an outlaw with a price on his head, David led the life of a Robin Hood on the desert frontier of his tribal domain in Judah (in the south of the Levant). He became the leader and organizer of a group of other outlaws and refugees, who progressively ingratiated themselves with the local population by protecting them from other bandits or, in case they had been raided, by pursuing the raiders and restoring the possessions that had been taken. Those actions eventually ensured that he would be "invited" to become king as the true successor of Saul after the latter was slain in battle against the Philistines on Mount Gilboa. According to the biblical account, David was proclaimed king in Hebron. He struggled for a few years against the contending claim and forces of Ishbaal, Saul's surviving son, who had also been crowned king, but the civil war ended with the murder of Ishbaal by his own courtiers and the anointing of David as king over all of Israel. He conquered the Jebusite-held town of Jerusalem, which he made the capital of the new united kingdom and to which he moved the sacred Ark of the Covenant, the supreme symbol of Israelite religion. Just like Elvis, he wanted to bring everyone of all creeds and religions together, David in a way did and is an important figure in Judaism, Christianity, and Islam. The Psalms are also attributed to him, a tribute to his legendary skill as a poet and hymnodist (composer).

Some scholars claim to have discovered artifacts that corroborate the biblical account of David's kingdom. Others assert that the archaeological record strongly suggests that David was not the grand ruler of a rising kingdom but merely a gifted tribal leader of a pastoral, rather than urban, society. David is a strong but unassuming shepherd who becomes God's choice to replace Saul as king of Israel. He is humble yet self-possessed, readily dismissing human opinion. His humility becomes clear early in his youth, when he kills the giant Goliath with a sling stone, declining the opportunity to use Saul's royal armour. Note they say he was humble just like Elvis, and just like Elvis also, David's mercy to others displays his selflessness—a product of his strenuous commitment to ethical ideals. It is also said that David is a young shepherd who gains fame first as a musician when you put all these things together you can see how like Elvis David was. It is also important to note how the name Jesse seems to follow Elvis around in different incarnations, so too the description of him being something of a Robinhood figure always giving to the poor and the needy.

https://en.wikipedia.org/wiki/David

WAS ELVIS ALEXANDER THE GREAT

In a past life one of the people Elvis might have been was Alexander the Great, not only does he resemble Elvis physically but he was also very musically talented and loved knowledge just as Elvis did, hence the library of Alexandria dedicated to him, we also know of Elvis's overwhelming draw to Egyptian, from calling Memphis his home although he was born in Tupelo, Memphis being the old capital of Egypt, and Alexander was once pharaoh of Memphis in Egypt and there is speculation he is buried there.

This is what has been said about Alexander the Great, so much of it resembles Elvis even what he looked like because as with some of the others Alexander had fair colouring as well.

"Despite his imperialist accomplishments ... has always seemed a melancholy figure, possessed by what ancient Greeks called pathos, a passionate yearning.," (Just like Elvis who had said he always felt alone and searched for his purpose)..He was a military genius and a hero to his men. He never asked them to do something he would not have done himself, and he bore the wounds to prove it. He also shared his vast riches with his men (just like Elvis). When he challenged his army to take the most difficult route, to do the impossible, they amazed themselves when they succeeded."

"He was the Sun God, the star of all time, Joe DiMaggio, Mickey Mantle rolled into one. Some historians put him...in a class with Genghis Khan and Attila the Hun, but they miss the point. No tyrant ever gave back so much. His life was not about money for himself, but about his growing curiosity, engaging and fulfilling his intellect, his consciousness, (again just like Elvis) was very religious. He reportedly stopped at all the major temples on his conquest route and made daily sacrifices to the gods. He had been raised to believe he descended from Achilles and Hercules. He had a deep respect for Zeus. These days we have a strong antipathy for conquerors, but in this time, war was a way of life and soldiering a much more honourable profession."

His temperance, as to the pleasures of the body, was apparent in him in his very childhood, as he was with much difficulty incited to them, and always used them with great moderation; though in other things be was extremely eager and vehement, and in his love of glory, and the pursuit of it, he showed a solidity of high spirit and magnanimity far above his age. For he neither sought nor valued it upon every occasion he lived thirty-two years and had reached the eighth month of his thirty-third year. He had reigned twelve years and these eight months. He was very handsome in person, and much devoted to exertion, very active in mind, very heroic in courage, very tenacious of honour, exceedingly fond of incurring danger, and strictly observant of his duty to the gods. In regard to the pleasures of the body, he had perfect self-control; and of those of the mind, praise was the only one of which he was insatiable. He was very clever in recognising what was necessary to be done, even when it was still a matter unnoticed by others; and very successful in conjecturing from the observation of facts what was likely to occur. In his haste, 'someone' left much of his family behind including his mother, wife, infant son and two daughters, our man ordered that they be "honoured, and addressed as royalty, "Although ... was stubborn and did not respond well to orders from his father, he was open to reasoned debate. He had a calmer side—perceptive, logical, and calculating. He had a great desire for knowledge, a love for philosophy, and was an avid reader. This was no doubt in part due to 'someone's' tutelage; .... was intelligent and quick to learn. His intelligent and rational side was amply demonstrated by his ability and success as a general. He had great self-restraint in "pleasures of the body." He had great charisma and force of personality, characteristics which made him a great leader. (Just like Elvis).

This man was also an accomplished musician had long fair wavy hair, could not or did not like to grow a beard and what is described as melting eyes, he also brought all those he conquered together something no one else could do, he is also the first man to be depicted with sideburns and was also the Pharaoh of

Memphis in Egypt. How much more could someone sound like Elvis, he had naturally blonde hair with a wave in it, like Vernon's hair, melting eyes, how often have we read people saying this about Elvis, and always clean shaven, when Elvis had to grow a beard for his part in Charro, he hated it and said he would never do it again.

"Alexander the Great of Macedon. In 334 BCE at the age of twenty-two, he and his army crossed the Hellespont and embarked on a decade-long journey to conquer the Persian Empire. As a supposed descendant of Achilles, Alexander believed his final victory over King Darius III was his destiny. By the time of his death in 323 BCE, he was convinced that he was not the son of King Philip II but, instead, was the son of the omnipotent Greek god Zeus.' This also ties in with Elvis who believed in later life that he had been Jesus in a previous incarnation.

I am sure as I can be Elvis was Alexander the Great, who the great library of Alexander was of course named after, fittingly as we all know how Elvis loved books, it has been said he had over a thousand in his library, maybe not as many the Great Library of Alexander, but an impressive amount that showed his thirst for knowledge.

https://www.worldhistory.org/article/925/alexander-the-great-as-a-god/?fbclid=IwAR09akAnW3Pg78azi_O0PJC5VSh7K6ri4nSCFnyBtT1QuV4F45t8Egnp1co

https://factsanddetails.com/world/cat56/sub366/entry-6170.html?fbclid=IwAR0J2e9oJDH9VTE1Q2LLUAUfgglq7yVfWBha8ANN9dCBpcn-7ka_pMjjm8Y

https://newyorkessays.com/essay-character-analysis-of-alexander-the-great/?fbclid=IwAR0EdQ7KNByQdJ9INgu5NyNeJ8Cc-0TlhAuw7IDLGUPkCOMbLJG_mWnd4Mw

https://www.livescience.com/39997-alexander-the-great.html?fbclid=IwAR2e4VbVLbZH9QCq6JIrC6HqauXeTBujqOOoYJwLaWFzBPR_i2UB3LwG5E8

http://www.alexandersgrave.com/alexanders-character/?fbclid=IwAR3SPcsUVfv900comDKabQSQEbL3uTmlqRugN8WzDop7xFliHB0-v2sulag

Although this may not at first glance look like Elvis, he has the same colour flaxen hair as Elvis and notice to the long fingers and toes like Elvis, and the flamboyant dressing.

To me these photos could not look more like
Elvis, the
likeness
between Elvis
Alexanders
mask could
hardly be
greater, this
mask looks like
it has been
made for Elvis.

WAS ELVIS MARCUS ANTHONY

Although Elvis has had many lives since, this life was still very much a part of him as Elvis, he loved all things Egyptian and often had his ex-es wear Cleopatra type eye make-up, in fact Elvis himself wore it especially in the early days, I have also been told he would like his ex-es to dress up and do the dance of the seven veils, I personally think there are many traits Elvis and Marus share.

Marcus first saw Cleopatra when she was 14 in Alexandria and was captivated even then by her beauty but would not see her again till she was in her 20s, by then she had become a lover of Ceasar's and had had a son to him by Caesarion, for a time she lived in Rome but she was not made to feel welcome there so returned to Egypt. Marcus was one of Ceasars most trusted soldiers, and it was he who uncovered who it had been who killed Ceasar.

Marcus was said to be loved by his soldiers and would prefer to spend time with the lower ranks than the higher. Marcus was also described as a passionate man who loved music and the arts, he was also considered brave and noble. Marus was also a Capricorn as Elvis was, Marcus was born 14th January 83 B.C. (don't forget these dates go backwards). After Ceasar was murdered three people in effect ruled Rome, Marcus, Lepidus and Octavian, between the three there was a great strain for who was the most powerful so to avert war, Marus married Octavian sister Octavia, his second wife after Fulvia died, (now what is curious about this, not only do the same people repeat and follow souls throughout their incarnations but so do names, Jesse has followed Elvis in several incarnations, and so too has Octavia, Gladys's mother Doll's real name was Octavia Luvenia Mansell. (To me this is very curious indeed and not a name you would associate with the time or place of Gladys's mother).

In 41B.C. Marcus summons Cleopatra to him in Tarsus, she is said to have entered the city by sailing up the Cydnus River in a decorated barge with purple sails, while dressed in the robes of the Greek goddess Aphrodite. Once again Marcus was totally besotted by her, in a piece I found it said that Marcus was so besotted by Cleopatra when he was away from her, he could not think straight for thinking of her, although originally their joining might have been political, I believe their love was true. I have also read that they would get dressed up as peasants so they could walk among their people and not be recognised.

Sadly, their love affair was not liked in Rome, together Marcus and Cleopatra had three children two of them fraternal twins, (again another big coincidence), fraternal twins Cleopatra Selene II and Alexander Helios, and another son named Ptolemy Philadelphus. In 31 B.C. Octavian declared that Marcus was an enemy of Rome and declared war on him and Cleopatra, (whether this had something to do with Marcus leaving his sister Octavia or just a power coup we do not know) and Octavian became Augustus Emperor of Rome. Marcus's and Cleopatras combined armies were defeated at the battle of Actium, now next there seem to be different accounts, some accounts say Marus defeated and knowing the torture that laid ahead for himself if taken back to Rome killed himself and on hearing of his death Cleopatra killed herself, a different account says they were both captured and Marcus was told Cleopatra was dead and so killed himself but she was not and his body was taken to her and with him dying in her arms she then killed herself. Whatever the truth of their deaths the fact remains neither could face life without the other their love was so strong.

https://www.ancient.eu/caesarion/

https://www.ancient.eu/article/197/cleopatra--antony/

https://en.wikipedia.org/wiki/Mark_Antony

https://www.biography.com/political-figure/mark-antony

https://www.history.com/topics/ancient-history/mark-antony

MARCUS

Cleopatra

WAS ELVIS KOOT HOOMI

In Ginger Alden's book she says Elvis tells her he thinks he was once a holy master called Koot Hoomi. She writes, "Elvis also admired David Andria's book "Through the Eyes of the Masters", which expounded on the belief that a person could reincarnate in another person's body. Over time, Elvis would tell me he thought Koot Hoomi, one of the masters from the book, was incarnated in himself, and pointed out a photo with the master dressed in a high-collared jacket similar to his own favourite style at the time."

"Elvis felt there was some force inside him, guiding him to teach and bring joy to others in various ways, especially through music. He was reading these books not only to understand his own life but to help others as well. Having witnessed some mystical things with Elvis already-and there would be more of these events ahead-I was beginning to wonder if the kinds of miracles we were reading about were possible. I wasn't ruling anything out."

AND THIS ABOUT KOOT HOOMI FROM WIKI
Koot Hoomi is said to be one of the Mahatmas that inspired the founding of the Theosophical Society. He engaged in a correspondence with two English Theosophists living in India, A. P. Sinnett and A. O. Hume, which correspondence

was published in the book The Mahatma Letters to A. P. Sinnett.

A quote attributed to Elvis: -"Be good, do no evil things to anyone or any living animal on this planet because if you do, you implant evil into your karma and sooner or later you will have to face it again in some form or other and it won't be any easier the next time. It's much easier to be good in the first place" Elvis Presley.

As most know Elvis was naturally blonde and Koot Hoomi is depicted with the same blonde hair and blue eyes that Elvis had.

Notice the striking eyes he has in this depiction; people have often said that about Elvis's eyes they thought he was looking into their souls.

WAS ELVIS JESSE JAMES

I know this may be hard for some people to believe maybe the one of the hardest, but there are several reasons why I believe Elvis was Jesse in a past life. I have had people say Elvis could never kill like Jesse did, but think on this, Frank is attributed with saying, "until that day Jesse was a kid who enjoyed the quiet things in life". That defining day I think tells us how much alike they are, we all know how protective Elvis was of his mother, imagine if someone blew up Elvis's mother as they did to Jesse's, Elvis would rain down hell on the person. They blew his home up, knowing Jesse was not there but knowing his mother was, she lost an arm in the explosion, if that wasn't enough they hung and rehung his step father to within an inch of his life trying to get him to say where Franks gang was, we all have the capability to kill given the right circumstances, and in those circumstances I could definitely see Elvis wanting to kill the perpetrator.

The name Jesse has followed Elvis in several past lives. The biblical Davids father was named Jesse, Elvis's own twin was called Jesse. Equally as strange is the aliver conspiracists think Elvis had another brother called Frank.

If you did not know you were reading about the infamous Jesse James it could quite easily be Elvis, they are describing. Jesse James was also known for his fascination with guns and had a parent who was a preacher, just like Elvis. Jesse has a compelling sense of himself as a spiritual being who is the searcher and the seeker of truth. That said, Jesse's life is devoted to investigations into the unknown, and finding the answers to the mysteries of life. Monumental as it is, Jesse is well-equipped to handle his mission. He enjoys a fine mind, and is an analytical thinker, capable of great concentration and theoretical insight. Jesse enjoys research, and putting the pieces of an intellectual puzzle together, and once he has enough pieces in place, Jesse is capable of highly creative insight and practical solutions to problems.

Jesse enjoys his solitude and prefers to work alone. He needs time to contemplate his ideas without the intrusion of other people's thoughts. He is a lone wolf and a person who lives by his own ideas and methods. As a result, close associations are difficult for Jesse to form and keep, especially marriage. Jesse needs his space and privacy, which, when violated, can cause him great frustration and irritation.

When his life is balanced, however, Jesse is both charming and attractive. He can be the life of a party and enjoys performing before an audience. Jesse loves displaying his wit and knowledge, which makes him attractive to others, especially the opposite sex. It should just be remembered that because he associates peace with the unobtrusive privacy of his world, intimacy is difficult for Jesse. It is Jesse's challenge to avoid shutting out the love of others and keeping him from experiencing the true joy of friendship and close companionship.

With his abilities to learn, analyse, and seek out answers to life's important questions, Jesse has the potential for enormous growth and success in life. By the time he reaches middle age, Jesse will radiate refinement and wisdom. Outwardly confident, but inwardly melancholy. Beneath the veneer of confidence and fearlessness lies a man deeply unsure of himself and completely unable to trust others. Oddly enough, Jesse is also obsessed with the media's depiction of him, he lives a life of quiet desperation he suffers through daily."

Jesse's father, Robert James, was a Baptist pastor and died when Jesse was just three years old. Robert was a man of learning and left behind fifty-one books in his will that dealt with math, chemistry, theology, astronomy, grammar, Latin, Greek, public speaking, philosophy, history, literature, and other subjects. Elvis's parents were lay-preachers, and another coincidence Elvis was also three when Vernon was sent to jail. Elvis himself had a vast library of books, many on the same subjects as Jesse did, and Elvis loved reading and sharing what he had learned with others.

In Elvis's first movie "Love Me Tender", Elvis plays the part of a young man too young to be a confederate soldier, just like Jesse was. Funny how life was repeated in art.

https://www.charactour.com/hub/characters/view/Jesse-James.The-Assassination-of-Jesse-James-by-the-Coward-Robert-Ford

https://www.abbevilleinstitute.org/was-jesse-james-a-southern-robin-hood/

In the coloured photo of Jesse, he has the same blue eyes as Elvis.

This is a
young Elvis
dressed as
a cowboy.

And this is a
young
Jesse
James

WAS ELVIS JESUS

Elvis believed in reincarnation and grew to believe he had been Jesus in a past life.
I know a lot of people will object to this but have an open mind and the possibilities which you may never have thought of, so please think before you condemn me for saying it. Thank you.
Elvis tried to be as Jesus like as he could in this life and as I have said he came to believe that he had been Jesus in a past incarnation.

When Elvis was seven years old his daddy Vernon took him in secret to see a comedy movie, it had to be in secret because the church they belonged to preached anything that was fun was a sin, and it had to be in secret cause Gladys would have whopped them both had she found out. Right then at the tender age of seven Elvis knew the church and religion was wrong, because he knew what Jesus preached/taught and he knew Jesus did not want everyone to be unhappy. So, Elvis started on his quest albeit in secret to be spiritual and not religious. Elvis knew what Jesus was, good, kind and humble and would help anyone he could, he knew Jesus did not distinguish one person from another, to him all were equal, man and woman no matter what their race, and we should treat everyone the same and help them as in the story of the Good Samaritan, he also knew Jesus never judged anyone, 'let him who is without sin cast the first stone'. All these things made perfect sense to Elvis, and so he tried his best to be like Jesus. He knew religion divided people and the church often grew rich out of their suffering, and that Jesus wanted everyone to be the same and that if religion really followed Jesus it would not have all the different denominations all squabbling with each other over who best worshiped god, and sadly sometimes they even went to war over it, and Elvis knew no loving good God would want this, neither would he want the churches to be dripping in gold, jewels and sacred objects while the people outside starved. Jesus always preached in the open and never inside, he had said that nature was God's cathedral, and you would find him under every stone, not in a temple.

So, Elvis tried as best he could to be like Jesus, to follow in his footsteps. Some people have accused me of putting Elvis on a pedestal of saying he was perfect, I know Elvis was not perfect, but he tried to be, in everything he did, it had to be the very best it could be, being good enough, was not being the best and being the best at what he did was what he always tried to be. Some people do not think Elvis was a good actor, but he was. When he was making some of those girly movies in the 60s he loathed them so much they made him physically ill to make them, as he himself said in an interview, but no one watching those movies would know it for one second because Elvis always did his best to be perfect, to give all he had, to make sure it was the best it could be, he literally tried to make silk purses out of sows ears, so was Elvis perfect, no, but he always tried to be, which is what made him so good at everything he did and made him better than most, because he tried to be like Jesus, not just pay Jesus lip service like so many do, they proudly say they are Christians and then do or say something totally against Jesus's teachings, I saw one say, they were nice to people who were nice to them, how is that being a Christian, Jesus said you should be nice to everyone, especially those who are not nice to you, for those you go the extra mile to try and include them in your flock, that person is not being the good shepherd that Jesus wanted us to be. Elvis understood this, so not only did he follow Jesus he also learnt about all the other religions and cultures of the world both current and ancient so he could better understand everyone on the planet, because like Jesus Elvis's greatest wish was to bring everyone together, had he of lived longer I think he might have managed it.

I know some people may not agree but Elvis's name is or was better known than anyone else by their first name and that included Jesus, why, because Elvis reached people in countries of all religions and into communist countries where the name of Jesus was never taught, in the early 60s people behind the iron curtain risked imprisonment to listen to Elvis on radios in their basements and learned English so they knew what he was singing, that is how great Elvis's power was, the power of love, and his love transcended all cultures all over the world, in all countries people know who Elvis is, there are Elvis impersonators in just about every country on the planet, and yet this man died over 45 years ago, who else could make such an impression in today's world, there have been books written about all those Elvis helped in their darkest hour, not only while he was alive but since his death, his love, his goodness, shines on even now and brings people from everywhere together, that is how great Elvis still is, was he perfect, no, but he was as perfect as a man could be given his circumstances and it was that vision he had, that love he gave unconditionally to everyone that is why he is still remember today.

Elvis strove to be like Jesus in every way he could and he did it well, Elvis came to believe he was Jesus in a previous life he saw the similarities between them and even called the MMs his disciples, he tried to make the world a better place and show people a better way of being as he had done when he was Jesus, he did it as perfectly as he could, given his circumstances and that is why you can find things like this, that people who are neither American, because Elvis's appeal was worldwide, and are not Christian, because Elvis transcended all beliefs by being as pure in heart as he could be, and by learning everything he could about everyone one and everything,

May 21, 1996 Web posted at: 6:15 p.m. EDT (2215 GMT) NEW DELHI, India (CNN) -- Maybe we can attribute all those Elvis sightings to reincarnation. In one small town in the Indian state of Karnataka, a picture of Elvis Presley hangs beside pictures of Hindu gods in a temple, according to a report in India Today magazine.

This is a testimony to how great Elvis was and is because as a small boy he decided to know Jesus and follow him, and to become spiritual, not religious.

We all know Elvis believed in reincarnation and he was a very old soul and how knowledgeable and wise he could be. We have also expressed the similarities between his life and that of Jesus's and there has been some discussion about what Jesus actually looked like and why he is always portrayed as being fair-haired and blue-eyed, well I found a letter on the internet that is supposed to have been written by Pontius Pilate about Jesus, and apparently Jesus was fair-haired and blue-eyed and not like a Jew according to Pilate, but like the Nazarian of Judea, so it is not beyond comprehension that Elvis a natural blonde, could have been Jesus in a previous incarnation, there is evidence of blonde people migrating to those lands thousands of years ago. The MMs said he called them his disciples and, in the video (link at the bottom) this man says Elvis told Larry Geller that he thought he may have been Jesus.

The Jesus of the Gnostic texts, the dead sea scrolls and Nag Hammadi are very different to those that Constantine had put in the New Testament bible which he had done as a political gambit to bring all the different religious factions of Rome together which is why all the feast days are in fact pagan, because he wanted everyone believing the same thing so they would be easier to rule, don't forget then Rome ruled most of the world, even Peters and Jesus's own gospels were left out because they did not fit in with Constantine's agenda, like the gospel where Jesus said his god was not the god of the Jews and that his god would crush their god, (the waring Jehova/Yahweh/ Allah god of the Jews most people pray to) and only then could peace reign, can you imagine if that had been added.

So is it possible that Elvis was Jesus in a past incarnation, read what Pontius Pilate had to say, this is just part of it the link to read the rest is below. I have been told since that this letter is now considered a forgery, but many things are, one day real the next day not, and back again as with the Shroud of Turin, so take what you will from the letter: -

This is a reprinting of a letter from Pontius Pilate to Tiberius Caesar describing the physical appearance of Jesus. Copies are in the Congressional Library in Washington, D.C.

To Tiberius Caesar:
A young man appeared in Galilee preaching with humble unction, a new law in the Name of the God that had sent Him. At first, I was apprehensive that His design was to stir up the people against the Romans, but my fears were soon dispelled. Jesus of Nazareth spoke rather as a friend of the Romans than of the Jews. One day I observed in the midst of a group of people a young man who was leaning against a tree, calmly addressing the multitude. I was told it was Jesus. This I could easily have suspected so great was the difference between Him and those who were listening to Him. His golden coloured hair and beard gave to his appearance a celestial aspect. He appeared to be about 30 years of age. Never have I seen a sweeter or more serene countenance. What a contrast between Him and His bearers with their black beards and tawny complexions! Unwilling to interrupt Him by my presence, I continued my walk but signified to my secretary to join the group and listen. Later, my secretary reported that never had he seen in the works of all the philosophers anything that compared to the teachings of Jesus. He told me that Jesus was neither seditious nor rebellious, so we extended

to Him our protection. He was at liberty to act, to speak, to assemble and to address the people. This unlimited freedom provoked the Jews -- not the poor but the rich and powerful.

Remember Elvis did have golden hair, not black. Elvis did in life see the similarities he had to Jesus, as I have said he even called the 'Memphis mafia' his disciples and apparently told Larry he thought he might have been Jesus and just like Jesus in the end he was betrayed by those closest to him. I know some will say that Jesus was the son of God so Elvis could not be him, but does not the bible say we are ALL CHILDREN of god, not just Jesus.

There is also evidence in the bible and Talmud that a Roman soldier named Pantera was in fact Jesus's biological father. Curiously Elvis owned a car called a Pantera, and his first karate name was panther, and Pantera means panther, Elvis only changed to tiger with the rise of the political group the black panthers. So, the name panther or Pantera has followed Elvis from his life as Jesus to Elvis.

Also please consider the fact that Elvis was a healer he cured Sylvia Shemwell's cancer, she was one of his backing singers. Elvis had a tremendous aura that many have attested to, just like Jesus would have, Elvis was also telepathic and telekinetic, and he could control the weather something else many saw, Elvis had many special powers just like Jesus would have had, several of those close to Elvis thought he was the second coming, no one else comes even close, but most importantly Elvis thought he had been Jesus.

https://www.timesofisrael.com/anomalous-blue-eyed-people.../

https://www.youtube.com/watch?v=mex9owS4zwY&feature=share...

https://en.wikipedia.org/.../Tiberius_Julius_Abdes....

https://blogs.timesofisrael.com/panteras-prodigy/

https://www.youtube.com/watch?v=M0HMXTP3vOs

https://www.allaboutreligion.org/gnostic-gospels.htm...

Artists often give Jesus blue eyes and flaxen hair like Elvis's real colouring.

How Elvis might of looked as Jesus.

BABY BIRD

As you all know Elvis believed in reincarnation and I believe I have in the past spent some of those lives with him, and this is one of them, I don't remember all of this life, so I guess you could call what I do remember the highlights from that life. This life takes place somewhere in the orient, like China or Japan, I do not know where exactly because that kind of knowledge was never told to someone like me, but it was a feudal society.

As many were there in those days I was given to the Master of the land my parents lived on as part payment, I don't remember them at all, or if they had given me a name, all I knew was I swept and scrubbed and mopped and cleaned out animal sheds and if I was anywhere near my Master when he was in a bad mood he would take it out on me. One day the other servants/slaves were abuzz that another Master was coming to see ours, ours had recently lost in a fight with this other Master and some bartering would be going on so he didn't have to give up any lands. The next thing I knew was I was hustled into the back of a wagon along with rolls of silk and rugs, they had not been tied up very well, so they kept on falling on me. A deal had been made and I was part of it. The journey seemed to take hours and was very bumpy, but of course I had no way of really knowing how long, only that the shadows I could see through the opening were growing longer. When we arrived I was shown where to go, there was very little talking though, now you have to remember I was a child slave, I had no fancy clothes, I don't know when I had last washed, my hair was knotted and dirty as was the rest of me and suddenly all these beautiful women were standing around with all their make-up and silk gowns on pointing me the direction to go. Then I had a door pointed to me to go through, I had never actually been in the palace of my old Master, the child slaves were not allowed and even though I was pretty tall for a child no one had suspected my secret, that I had recently just become a woman, (I am sure you understand).

So I walked into this room with silk wall hangings and rugs and cushions on the floor, the likes of which I had never seen before, in the middle of the room was a man, the new Master, some of the other women had followed me in and he said in a booming deep voice for them to go and get water and clothes, which they did in what seemed like a split second, I have the feeling they had already had it all prepared for him. They came and settled the bowls of water down beside him; you could see the water was warm and it was covered in rose petals to make it smell sweet. Not knowing what was coming next. I have to say the deepness of his booming voice frightened me, I had heard stories about these Master's and what they did to girls and women. He beckoned me over to him, and I tried to walk as gracefully as the other women had, but it was no good, I couldn't, and felt a fool. He padded the cushion next to him and said "come", so I did and I as I knelt on the cushion in my rags, with a nod and flick of his hand all the others left the room. Now I was so frightened I was shaking, my head was down to my knees, I had no idea what was about to happen, and although I couldn't actually see him now, my face buried in my knees it was like I could feel the atmosphere in the room changing. He cupped my face in one of his hands and pulled me up so I was kneeling up and not down, then he started taking off my rags/clothes, he must have been able to feel me shaking and said, "You are like a frightened little bird shaking so much, so that is what I will call you, Baby Bird." For the first time in my life, I had an actual name to respond to. As he took my clothes off, I could see he was getting angry I thought I must displease him in some way, as he looked at my bruises he said in a softer almost trembling voice, "No one will ever hurt you again my Baby Bird, that Master was a brute, but you are mine now." Although I was much relieved, I still didn't know what I was supposed to be doing and I did not want to displease my new Master.

Then he started to do something I would never have believed in my wildest dreams, he started to bathe me with the water, I had thought it was me who was supposed to bathe him. He was so gentle as he caressed my face with the wet cloth getting all the dirt off and being ever so gentle on my bruises, then he leaned over and took a brush and brushed the knots out of my hair. Then he beckoned me to kneel up, fear spread through my body again I had been given to him as a child, but there was no way of hiding this, as I knelt up he saw the rags between my legs, and instead of being enraged as I thought he would, he got a half-smile on his face and said in a gentle deep velvety voice, "I don't blame you Baby Bird if I had been you I would not have wanted him to know either", he then bathed me down to my knees and told me to stand and bathed me all the way down to my feet, I couldn't believe it when he started at actually bathe my feet as well, I had for a woman from those parts long feet and toes and he seemed fascinated by them and bathed each toe separately, as I stood there I could see all the bowls of water were looking pretty dirty by now, I was looking down on him, it was something I could not get my head around, this warrior and Master of all these lands was kneeling down bathing my feet, I convinced myself I must have been hit really hard by one of the carpets in the wagon and I was actually unconscious or maybe even dead. As I stood there in a trance I was soon awakened when he clapped his hands together sharply as he put a large cloth around me, and then some of the beautiful women came in, I looked down to see the blood had been trickling down my legs, I guess he hadn't noticed it at first either, he waved his hand and the women

[277]

ushered me out of the room, it was like they had some kind of code or they knew what he was thinking.

They took me to another room and soon as I was being washed again, not gently this time and clean rags were put in place between my legs, my hair was combed till it shone, I didn't even know my hair could shine, make-up was put on my face and a silk dress and an over gown, layers of clothing were put on me. Then came my feet they all had tiny feet, ladies' feet, I had peasants' feet, eventually they found something that almost fitted me, well fitted me good enough and I was ushered back to be presented to my new Master. As I entered my Master's room all the others left, he was already in bed and patted his hand on the space next to him, 'you sleep here tonight', my heart was in my mouth I had heard stories about my old master and what he did to young women. He then asked me if I liked my new home to which of course I said "yes", he gave out a low kind of grunt turned his back and me and fell asleep. I lay there rigid all night on top of the covers terrified to move in case I woke him up and made him angry. In the morning a tray of food was brought in, and I was told to feed the Master, which I did, it was strange feeding a full-grown man and wiping his mouth for him like there was something wrong with him, but this is what he wanted so that was what I did. Just as he finished someone else came in and took me and the tray away, no words were spoken.

A week or more went by before I saw the Master again, in that time the other women tried to teach me how to dress, put my hair up and make-up on, these things where I was told essential if I wanted our Master to like or want me, he liked perfection in everything. So, this day I was dressed and had attempted to put my hair up as it should be, so I looked like all the others and was halfway through trying to put my make-up on when someone came in and whispered to the woman in charge of me. "The Master wants to see you now", "now" I replied, "go, you cannot keep the master waiting", I was ushered into the Master's room, the sunken bit in the middle had been filled with water and half a dozen women all sat in it with him laughing and giggling, about what I had no idea, but they seemed to be enjoying themselves. He must have heard the door close as he had his back to it, with a wave of his hand the women hastily got out of the bath/pool grabbed large cloths to wrap themselves in and their clothes and were gone. "Why are you still standing there" he said in a slightly agitated deep voice, he moved round to the other side of the bath so he could see me and started laughing, "oh I see they are teaching you how to do your hair and make-up" he said, I thought I must look like a clown to him, all the women have their hair and make-up done so precisely they all look identical. Seeing how nervous I was his tone changed and he told me to take my clothes off and get in, so I did and sat opposite him, the water was just the right temperature and covered in rose petals, never had I known such a thing before. "Why are you over there sit next to me" so reluctantly I moved round to sit beside him, immediately he had removed the pins in my hair and shook it lose, "there that's better", he said, "You have good hair, you do not need to wear it up", so much for the other women saying we all had to look the same I thought, then he took a small cloth dampened it in the water and proceeded to remove the thick make-up I had tried so hard to get right. "You have good skin and are beautiful you don't need make-up" he said, then whispering in my ear he said, "Some of the women they need make-up without it they are ugly", and he laughed a hearty laugh and I laughed too, the tension was broken, this man was not the man the other women had told me he was.

Every now and then he would clap his hands loudly, the first time frightened the life out of me, which he also found funny, and someone would run in with jugs of hot water. For what seemed a few hours he told me of his exploits as a warrior, some quite funny, and when he laughed so did I, I could tell he was a very proud man but there was a softness under all his bluster. Suddenly he rose up out of the water, it hadn't occurred to me that he wouldn't have any clothes on, and I had never seen a naked man before, I didn't know where to put my eyes and even though I was trying not to look I could see he was tall lean and muscular, the layers of clothes he wore had made him look heavier than he actually was. "Don't just sit there dry and clothe me", he said sharply, then he noticed my nervousness and started to laugh again, "Oh you've never seen a man with no clothes before have you", I shook my head, 'Well this man is getting cold, hurry up", so that is what I did as quickly as I could and trying not to look as I was doing it. Then he said, "I want to show you something so be quick", as quickly as I could I got dressed, I didn't dare spend time drying myself, he said be quick so quick it had to be.

As he walked out of the room I shuffled along behind him, suddenly he stopped and turned his head to look at me and started laughing again, "Baby bird with big boots and wet hair", I didn't think it was that funny but the sight of me amused him and he had remembered the name he had given me, so that was a plus. Soon we came to another room, he slid the door open and in unison all those inside turned their heads round to look, the room had twenty or more children all sat on the floor all different ages from toddler to those about to become men and women, even a baby was in the arms of one of the older ladies who sat facing the others, (they had grey hair), all together they all said hello father. "These are all my children," he said proudly puffing his chest out, I now understood the need for all the women he had. He said, "my sons will grow up to be warriors and my daughters will be consorts and marry other landowners like me who border our land, so we have peace."

He then left the room and I followed, one of the women then brought a tray filled with all sorts of food, most I had never seen before, she handed me the tray to carry and off she went. "I want to eat in the garden, come," he said, so I dutifully followed my Master, it was a beautiful garden, there was a pool at each end with a stream running between and a little bridge going over it and it had plenty of fish in it. He sat on the grass near the stream and patted the ground for me to sit next to him. I knelt beside him, he sat crossed legged and I started to feed him as I had done the other morning, after he had had a few mouthfuls he asked if I was hungry and as I opened my mouth to reply he popped a berry of some kind in my mouth, I thought I must be dreaming, the Master was feeding me, no one would believe me I thought if I told them. And so, it went on till we had both had enough, we fed each other. Then in a serious but soft voice he said, "I want a number one son," I did not understand he had lots of sons surly the oldest would be his number one son. He continued, all those women, my concubines were supposed to be pure when they came to me, but they had been trained from birth what to say and what not to say and really I do not trust any of them, so were they pure when they were given to me, "you", he said "you I know are, as you had hidden your womanhood, so I know if you have my son it will have to be mine and no one else's", I wasn't sure if I should be happy or sad at this, basically I thought to myself he wanted to use me, it also struck me what a sad life he must have, not to know who he could trust, for me it was easy I had never trusted anyone I couldn't if I wanted to survive, I had always had to be on my guard so to speak.

The Master stood up and said "Come", and beckoned me to follow, so I did. After a short walk up a hill we came to the top, there he stopped and spread out his arms and proudly said, "This is all my land as far as you can see, and one day it will be my number one son's, so you can see it is important that I can be sure he is mine and mine alone". He then pointed to the land immediately below us where I could see food growing in the fields and animals, much like the ones I used to clean up after. Then he turned to me and said "None of the people who live on my land have to pay me the way your parents did, none of them will ever have to give me their children because they have no other way of paying", and he gave me a long deep look which I wasn't sure of, then he continued, " People who live on my land come and tend my crops for one or two days a week, that is how they pay me", he went on to explain that even his warriors had to spend time tending the animals and crops, " that way they know what and who they are fighting for and it builds different strength than warrior training", I was starting to see a different side of this man, a side I thought he must keep hidden from most, then he totally surprised me by saying, "sometimes I go down and work in the fields", I looked at him quizzically, " I told you I cannot trust anyone up here, they only tell me what they think I want to hear, so I put on old rags and go down there and talk to my people and listen to them, they do not know it is me, so they tell me the truth, they tell me if something is wrong, if someone has mistreated them, or if one of them needs a doctor, I never tell anyone how I know these things, my advisors must think I have special powers" and he laughed, but I could see this man truly cared for his people. The people on his land who were under his protection, and I wondered at the irony that had brought us together, if my parents Master had been as good as this one was, we would never have met.

When we got back to his room there was a line of his women waiting for him to choose one, with a flick of his wrist he dismissed them all except the one who seemed in charge, he told her from now on he wanted me and only me to be his companion till he said otherwise, she nodded and went. I wasn't really sure what this meant, then he said," all those women have been trained from birth to only say what they think I want to hear, if they speak at all, most of the time they just nod in agreement", he said, then he said "you have no training you are like an uncut gem so you will be who I want you to be", now I wasn't sure if I was happy with that but at least I wasn't scrubbing the floor of the animal shed so I figured it must be a win. That evening he spent most of the time talking to me telling me how he thought things should be or reading to me from a book, then he declared that I needed to learn the art of reading and writing so I could read to him, and we could discuss things better. He then said if he asked me for my opinion, he wanted me to give him an honest answer not just nod, because it infuriated him, he had enough people who did that and would then go and talk about him behind his back, or they thought it was behind his back, he said he always got to know everything everyone said. I wasn't sure if that was a warning or a statement of fact. Eventually we both fell asleep; the next day was very similar to the day before except he told one of the older women where the children were that she had to tutor me in the art of reading and writing and other things. This took place for about an hour a day, or at least the duration the candle said, some days when the Master had meetings with his advisors or generals, I would be with her all day or however long the meeting took place. As the months carried on, I became fond of my Master, he was always gentle with me and treated me well.

Some of the other women were not happy with this arrangement but others were. After many months of being the master's sole companion I realised my monthly bleed had stopped so I mentioned it in passing to the woman who was teaching me to read and write, occasionally we even did some painting, she said I was better at that than the writing. She got quite an extraordinary look on her face and said, "stupid girl you have his child in your belly, he won't want you in his bed now with a big fat belly", at this point she marched me back to the Master's room and announced to the Master that I was carrying his child and then said, "I'll take her back to the women's room". Well she got that one so wrong, you never tell the Master you ask, when I saw the rage coming over his face and his hands clenched into fists at his side I wasn't sure if he was angry at her for speaking to him in such a way or at me for having his baby in my belly without telling him, but his rage was for her, he virtually growled at her through clenched teeth, "she is MY companion and I say what she does". With that she hurried out of the room as fast as her shuffling feet could carry her. Then he turned to me, he sat down on the edge of his bed, normally we sat on the floor and beckoned me to sit next to him, "from now on" he said, "I do not want you to leave my side, I do not want anything to happen to my number one son", thanks I thought, it wasn't me he was concerned for after all.

The next months passed quite quickly, and I was surprised by the amount of attention my Master was giving me, though I was never sure if he was giving me all this attention for me or because I was carrying his child, he seemed to be putting so much on this child being a boy it frightened me what would happen if it was a girl. The day finally arrived when my waters broke, I was quickly taken to a room with doctors and some of the older women in. He did not come with me. When the baby was born, to my relief it was indeed a boy, one of the women helpers put it straight to my breast to suckle while they cut the cord then they wrapped his stomach then wrapped him a cloth then a silk cloth and took him to my Master, I wondered if I would ever see my son again. A short while went by and I was trying to hear what the doctors and women were whispering about, were they were discussing what to do with me, normally I would be taken back to where all the other women were, and I would be given three months to get back in shape. As I was wondering what would happen to me if I didn't get back into shape the door slid open and in walked the Master carrying his number one son, my son. He came over to me and softly said "You have done well Baby Bird, I am pleased with you", then he turned to the others in the room and sharply said "Why isn't she in my room, do you expect her to walk", with that they hurriedly picked up the bed with me on it and took me to his room and set the bed down beside his bed. Again, in an angry voice he said,

"And do you expect her to climb onto my bed by herself, she has just had my number one son", so they lifted me and the thin mattress up onto his high bed and then they all scurried out of the room. He then started to laugh, I had no idea why and he then told me never had any of the other mothers been allowed back to his room so quick and the look on their faces amused him. He then gave me back the baby and told me he was hungry and asked did I know how to feed him, at that moment an older women came in, his sister, I had seen her before and he had told me she had had an accident as a child and the doctors had said she should never get pregnant so she was never married but stayed with him and looked after his children instead, he naturally thought she had an idyllic life looking after all his children, and maybe she did in a way. A small bed was also brought in and set down on the other side of the room and a smaller bed/cot for the baby. My Master told me she would stay with us from now on so she could teach me how to look after his most precious number one son, I really wasn't sure if I liked this idea or not. He proclaimed she would do everything for me, it also meant we had no privacy, which for the first few months was a good thing, I had no idea how tired I would be and how demanding looking after my Master and a baby would be, so I was grateful she was there.

As time went on our son grew into a strong boy and young man, and my Master dotted on him and to the surprise of everyone else he dotted on me too, he said I had been the only person he had ever felt totally comfortable with. Our son soon became a young man and the dance lessons he took had turned into the art of fighting and he became a warrior like his father, my Master. As I suspect all mothers feel, half of me was proud of him and half worried that he would get hurt. My Master had made it clear to everyone from the second he was born that one day he would take over from the Master and rule his lands, so when he got old enough he was expected to take a wife from neighbouring lands to bring more peace, but being my son he didn't want to marry a consort, he wanted to marry a peasant girl as I had been and as it happened one of the lands neighbouring ours had always had to pay my Master for use of one of his streams that went on to his land because this Master could not no matter how hard he tried have any girl babies, so my son chose one of the peasant girls from his land on the understanding that they first made the girl his daughter, otherwise she would be like me and not allowed to actually marry my son, but just be his concubine, and so it happened, our number one son married a peasant girl who was adopted so she could be a consort and not a concubine. Life went on as it does and I got on well with my son's wife, every time they went to battle, we would sit there our hearts in our mouths waiting for my sons return. For some reason I had never worried about my Master, I guess he had been doing it so long it had just become part of what he did. As we sat there this day waiting for their return, we heard the horses being ridden hard back to the palace, normally at the end of a battle they would be brought back slow so they could rest more. Suddenly my son slid open the door and shouted for me to be quick and I raced to my Masters room, the other men there walked out as I raced in, my Master was laying on the cushions on the floor, I kneeled down and cradled him in my arms, "I am done for" he said in a quiet voice, he cupped his hand around my face as he had done so many times before and pulled me down to his face and whispered to me words I had always known but that had never been spoken in that velvety voice of his, "I have always loved you Baby Bird", "and I you", I said softly in return, and I saw that half smile of his cross his face, his hand dropped from my face and his body went limp, without even thinking about it I took his dagger from its sheath and plunged it into my heart and slumped over his body. People think death is instantaneous, but it is not, I must have let out a yell, for at that second, I heard the sound of men's heavy boots once again entering the room. What I can only describe as a warm glow seemed to fill my body and the next thing I knew I was up on the ceiling with my Master, looking down on our son who lifted my body up just enough to remove the dagger then laid me back down on top of my

Master, he then gave his first order as the new Master, "I want them to be buried like that together in each other's arms, so they will always be together".

I always think Elvis has an oriental look to him in this photo.

CHAPTER FOUR

Quote attributed to Vernon.

"MY BOY MY BOY, THEY'VE KILLED MY BOY".

ELVIS WAS MURDERED

Vernon always believed Elvis had been murdered, so much so when the coroner's report could not find out why Elvis's heart had stopped but announced his findings in such away the average person mistakenly thought Elvis had had a heart attack. Vernon had his own autopsy performed on Elvis, in the hopes of finding the cause of Elvis's heart stopping. This report has been locked away till 2027, fifty years after Elvis's death, from what I have read and been told this was to protect Elvis's relatives that were still living.

Not content with the investigation into his son's death and the way it was quickly wrapped up leading the public to think it was natural causes, Vernon started his own investigation, at the time the authorities were frightened of rioting that might happen if it had been anything but natural, and cancelled all police leave, this I believe is why Elvis's murder was covered up. I hope to show here that Elvis was indeed murdered just as Vernon said. We might find out exactly what Vernon found out in 2027, if his findings are with the autopsy and are made public, what I do know is Vernon was frightened enough for his family he felt he could not go to the authorities because he was not sure who he could trust as

Donna Presley said in her book 'Precious Memories'.

OFFICIAL STORY

We are supposed to believe that Elvis was straining on the toilet when he had a massive heart attack and fell off the toilet sideways, landing on his face, breaking his cheekbone and nose with his butt in the air and his PJ pants down.

The toilet had no evidence in it that Elvis had been on it at all. Having fell off the toilet, the evidence was his P.J. pants were down, he is said to have fallen so heavily on his face that he broke his cheekbone and nose. The carpet was a thick shag pile carpet, and it is hard to believe he fell sidewards onto his face with his butt in the air, an impossible task I would have thought for anyone, even Elvis.

Elvis is also supposed to have thrown his book, which they changed the title of it, it was actually "Sex and Psychic Energy by Betty Bethards" against the door to get someone's attention, but he was already at the door as the toilet is right next to the door. We are also told he crawled through his own vomit, pretty clever for a dead person who had landed on his face from the toilet next to the door and stayed there.

The EMTs said the counter on the opposite wall was also in disarray, with everything knocked over like there had been a fight, weird considering Elvis had a heart attack on the toilet and then fell off sideways landing on his face with his butt in the air.

We had no need to be told that he had his PJ pants down, they said it to make it look like he had fallen off the toilet, when if anything it shows he had crawled along the carpet for some way, as anyone who has tried to crawl on a thick shag pile carpet will tell you it drags whatever you have on down, especially something silky, like Elvis's pyjamas, and the fact they also said he crawled through his own vomit also makes a mockery of the toilet theory, as does Elvis throwing his book towards the toilet door, how could he have of, if he was already at the door. Unfortunately, most people never bother to check to see if the story matches the facts if it is told by someone in authority and written down, as in this case where the facts do not match up to the official story at all, in fact they make a mockery of each other and rely on the people reading it to not use their own common-sense. I hope I can show you in this chapter what really happened that day.

ELVIS'S HEALTH

Elvis had a physical every year for his insurance with "Lloyds of London", he talks about the one he had in 76 in the Red West phone call, and he passed the one in 77 also.

These pseudo autopsy programs on TV do not have access to Elvis's medical records or autopsy any more than we do, all they do is sensationalise to get people to watch, they do not care about the truth, only ratings, I have heard some stupid things said on those programs, like Elvis's intestines were twice as long as they should have been, firstly it is impossible and secondly we know Elvis had barium meal in his intestines at time of death, the ONLY reason for that is because he had had an x-ray, within the last two weeks before he died, of his intestines, quite possibly as part of the physical for Lloyds, and if there had been any problem with his intestines at that time they would have seen it and done something about it, but there was not, they were fine. The other one that is often quoted and is also rubbish is Elvis's heart was twice the size it should have been, when Elvis had the physical, they had him running on a treadmill while he was attached to a heart monitor, and they found nothing seriously wrong with his heart.

Do not forget Elvis was an athlete, the stage suits he wore with the silky sleeves, had those sleeves because they weighed so much, some weighed 75lbs, now you must be an athlete to be able to sing and dance wearing those. Just as with all athletes his heart would have been bigger than an average heart, it is a muscle and like all muscles the more they are worked the bigger they get, just like his lungs were bigger than average because he was a singer. When Elvis had his physical, they had him running on a treadmill while wired up to an ECG machine, had there been anything wrong with his heart it would have showed up then, so please do not believe these programs, use your common sense and think about it, if you have any knowledge of anatomy you know I am right. Yes, Elvis did have problems he took medication for, and these are all he had, don't forget he was out riding his Harley Davidson motorbike two days before his death, a heavy bike that you need to be fit to manoeuvre, and the night before he died, we are told he was playing racquetball, if he had heart problem he could not have.

Elvis had medication for: -
Viral Arthritis, back then it was called Reiter's syndrome and being double-jointed/hypermobile it exacerbated it and was possibly the cause of his other ailments like Migraines, Glaucoma, and Insomnia, although he had suffered with insomnia for most of his life as well, but Reiter's would have exacerbated it.

In Dr Nicks book he said he once withdrew Elvis's sleep meds thinking he would eventually fall asleep naturally, but after about 4 days and nights without sleep Dr Nick knew it was not something Elvis just took on a whimsy like some would have you believe, but that he needed sleep meds, it is also quite possibly the Reiter's was the reason his joints and bones ached so much I would think.

He had also suffered from constipation all his life which occasionally resulted in his colon twisting due to lazy bowel, (Lisa has also inherited a lazy bowel too,) it was not something that just happened in the 70s.

Diabetes, (due to a diet Elias Ghanem had Elvis on).

Hypertension. (Who wouldn't have with all stress like Elvis was under)

Elvis also always since childhood had sleepwalked which is why he was supposed to be checked on all the time, he also had nightmares every time he slept all his life and suffered from depression which got much worse in the 70s.

So PLEASE DO NOT BELIEVE these pseudo-scientific programs they are all bogus.
In case you are wondering I have a diploma in anatomy and physiology, so I do know a bit about how the body works.

CARDIAC ARRHYTHMIA

I must state right here and now no way did Elvis die of cardiac arrhythmia, the fact is this, you cannot diagnose this on someone who is dead, you must listen to the heart to diagnose this, so if you have seen a program or read a book which says this is why Elvis died, they are lying. Elvis had a medical for Lloyds of London two weeks before his death and in that medical they had him running on a treadmill for between five to ten minutes, had Elvis had cardiac arrhythmia it would have shown then, but it did not, I do wish people would use their own common sense before believing what someone has written in order to sell a book or get viewer ratings.

https://www.medilexinc.com/a-spoonful-of-medicine-blog/fatal-arrhythmias-diagnosing-post-mortem?fbclid=IwAR13rKhwP2XMOyU5UfFs8K-mrBLznVOG-yv4K0j6KgIA7Tu8MDZY5B-dtvo#:~:text=In%20fact%2C%20the%20only%20way,death%20in%20a%20legal%20proceeding

SYRINGES

We know Elvis had twenty times the normal amount of codeine in his bloodstream, and that Elvis was allergic to codeine. We also know he showed many signs of strangulation, but these signs also are often the same in anaphylactic shock, which it says about in the autopsy that Vernon had sealed according to Donna Presley's book.

When someone is strangled or goes into anaphylactic shock, several things happen as they die, their eyes bulge, they bite down that hard on their tongue, they can even bite through it, and in men their genitals enlarge. Elvis almost bit through his tongue but not quite, his eyes were bulging and apparently his gentles enlarged, and Elvis also had blood in his nostril as well.

The detective Dan Warlick said he found two cartridge-type syringes in the bathroom, and this is important, neither of them had any cartridge in them or a needle either. He said he checked over Elvis's body for any puncture marks and did not find any. That type of syringe is the type that is used to go into soft tissue, like a dentist uses, now Dan Warlick could not have possibly checked inside Elvis's mouth because rigor mortice had set in and as I said Elvis had bitten down on his tongue, so even if someone had injected Elvis in the mouth it would have been obscured. The detective did not say if he had shone a light up Elvis's nose, only that there was blood and carpet fibres there, so once again, the injections could have taken place there. Neither did he say if he had checked any other soft tissue areas like deep into the ear, or in Elvis's gentles which would explain the trousers being down as well.

There is no possible way that Elvis could have injected himself as he would have gone into shock almost immediately and not been able to remove the empty cartridges and needles and dispose of them somewhere other than the bathroom, so someone else must have done it. Warlick did say he thought the syringes might have been left there to make people think Elvis had accidentally overdosed, but that would have been impossible, because no way could Elvis have tidied up after himself. When Elvis was first given codeine in the army he found it immediately hard to breath, so with twenty times the therapeutic dose in his system he would have been fighting for breath and his life straight away, so if nothing else convinces you Elvis was murdered this should.

I do not know which type of cartridge syringe Dan Warlick found he did not say, but this is what they tend to look like.

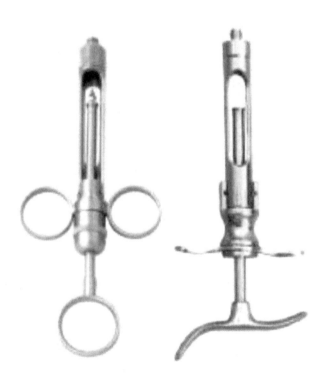

LIVIDITY

Lividity is the pooling of blood after a person dies. Once the heart stops pumping the blood around the body gravity takes over and takes all the blood to the lowest part of the body, but not to any part of the body that is being constricted by tight clothing or an object, such as the floor. So if you died sitting up in a chair the blood would pool into your lower legs, and top of your feet but not the bottom of your feet if they were in contact with the ground, because the blood would not be able to get there, similarly if you had tight restricting socks on to just under your knee lividity would only start after the sock around the knee. It is also important to know the colour of the lividity because different colours can mean different things, like poisoning, or hyperthermia.

We know from Joe that Elvis died with his butt in the air and that he had crawled through his vomit in an attempt to get to the door, we also know from the EMTs that according to them the room looked like there had been a fight there, they said everything was in disarray, they also said and this is crucial, that Elvis was so dark they thought he was a black man, which might be very significant. Everything I can find online says that this is a sign of poisoning, most articles online say it is a sign of nitrate poisoning. "High levels of methaemoglobin can be noted at necropsy due to the presence of a chocolate-brown discoloration of the blood in about one-half of the cases of nitrate poisoning.".". The only other reason for this discolouration I can find is Clostridium Perfringens, which is like a stomach bug that causes diarrhoea, and we know Elvis did not have diarrhoea and it is a bug usually caught from undercooked meat, which we can be pretty sure Elvis did not eat because he liked his meat very well done. So, everything I can find on the net says it is nitrate poisoning.

It is also important to remember that Elvis had carpet fibres in his nose, I think this means they must of held his face into the carpet while he struggled for his last breath and kept it there till they were sure Elvis was dead, then when they let go, his face came off the carpet slightly allowing the blood to pool in his face, causing him to look like a black man. The other curious thing is this, if Elvis had been crawling and just died then one knee would have been in front of the other and he would have slumped to his side, and the lividity would not have then been in his face, I think after he died they must have moved his knees to form a sort of 'A' form structure to keep him balanced so he did not fall to the side, if you kneel on the floor with one knee in front of the other as if crawling, with your head down, but not quite touching the floor and your butt in the air and then release all the tension in your muscles, completely relax as if dead, you will fall to the side, but Elvis did not, so they must have positioned him specifically to keep him in that position, with his head down and butt in the air, I have been told it is the way a person who has been hit by the mob is left, otherwise he would have slumped and his face would have been to one side, very rarely would anyone stay like this naturally, in fact I would say it would almost be impossible. It was not till he was found that they then turned him on to his side.

Now I do not know how much was known back then about lividity and its colouration, but I am pretty sure today it would not be so easy to cover this up as it was then, the big question being is why didn't they suspect anything from the colour of the lividity and test for it, no they only tested for drugs cause someone wanted it to look like he had overdosed when we know from the toxicology report he did not. Please note the sketch I have done showing the position of Elvis's body from what we have been told, and also please check out the links I have provided if you wish to know anything more about lividity or nitrate poisoning which generally only happens to farmworkers, grazing animals and babies. Elvis was none of these, so I think one of the empty cartridges found at the scene might of been used to inject him with the nitrate just in case the codeine did not kill him.

https://www.poison.org/articles/causes-and-symptoms-of-nitrate-nitrite-poisoning-174

https://mlt.gov.np/post-mortem-changes/early-post-mortem-interval/post-mortem-lividity/

https://www.addl.purdue.edu/newsletters/2002/fall/nitrate.shtml

https://www.encyclopedia.com/social-sciences-and-law/law/crime-and-law-enforcement/lividity

https://www.sciencedirect.com/topics/medicine-and-dentistry/livor-mortis

https://www.osmosis.org/answers/lividity

Anaphylaxis

Vernon was convinced Elvis died of anaphylactic shock because of the amount of codeine in Elvis's blood when he died. Elvis first found out he was allergic to codeine when he was in the army, when he immediately found it hard to breathe after taking some, and so had never taken any since and everyone knew Elvis was allergic to codeine.

Vernon concluded someone had either swapped Elvis's meds or more likely they had injected Elvis with the codeine as two empty cartridge type syringes were found in the bathroom, the needles had also been removed and it would not have been possible for Elvis to have injected himself and then removed the cartridges and needles and disposed of them before the anaphylaxis had set in, which is practically immediate, so someone must have injected Elvis with them, directly to murder Elvis. Also codeine is notorious for making people vomit, so no way would Elvis of had enough time to digest any codeine pills and keep them in his stomach long enough for them to metabolise and get into his blood without vomiting them all up, Elvis did vomit as he was dying but this is more probably because of the effects of the anaphylaxis, which makes the tongue swell and gives the person a sensation of gagging hence the vomit. It is also highly likely Elvis was also strangled as well as both the anaphylaxis and strangulation have similar effects on the body, strangulation, as well as the obvious gagging feeling, also presents itself with a swollen tongue which is often bit through by the person as well as bulging eyes, which was also reported about Elvis's body, and I have been told the thick gold chain Elvis was wearing had cut into his neck. Because of the way the body decomposes it is very hard to detect anaphylaxis in a corpse as this study below has shown, so it is not surprising it was missed by the coroner.

"In many cases of fatal anaphylaxis no specific macroscopic findings are present at post-mortem examination. This reflects the rapidity and mode of death, which is often the result of shock rather than asphyxia. Investigations that might help determine whether anaphylaxis was the cause of death had rarely been performed. In the presence of a typical clinical history, absence of post-mortem findings does not exclude the diagnosis of anaphylaxis."

https://pubmed.ncbi.nlm.nih.gov/10823122/

HYOID BONE

The hyoid bone has one job in life to do and that is to anchor the tongue, it is not connected to any other bone, like most bones are, and it is a very fragile little V-shaped bone, which breaks very easily if someone is strangled. Elvis had all the outward signs of having been strangled, which are similar to anaphylaxis, he had almost bitten his tongue through, his eyes were protruding and had petechial haemorrhaging, and he had blood in his nose, yet as far as I am aware nowhere does it mention any inspection of the hyoid bone at all in the coroner's report, to me this seems extremely strange. Especially as it has been said they tried to find out why Elvis's heart stopped, yet this was not looked at, indeed they have tried to say these signs are because of his heart-stopping, which is pure nonsense. My father had heart attacks for seven years till they killed him and never did he bite his tongue. Those who are aware of what a hanged man looks like will know these signs are that of someone who has been strangled and not someone who has had a heart attack, and if your heart just stopped as Elvis's supposedly did you definitely do not get these signs, all of this conjecture could have been stopped with one simple observation, was the hyoid bone intact or had it been fractured, yet it was never mentioned. Did they find it had been broken and to stop rioting in the streets decided to hide it, it is beyond me how all these learned doctors did not even bother to look when the signs were so obvious.

HEART ATTACK

The pseudo-science and doctors try to sell to us is Elvis died of a heart attack because he had a blocked colon/intestine, this is utter rubbish, especially as Dr Fransico who was the coroner apparently said, "Elvis did not have an impacted colon at the time of his death." in a Memphis newspaper. You can die from pushing too hard if you burst a blood vessel especially in your brain, but NEVER, and I will say that again, NEVER have I heard such hogwash that someone's internal organs can push upwards and stop the heart from actually beating, which is what they try to sell to us happened, I am going to say right here as far as I am concerned that is impossible, and if someone has experience of this happening then please do correct me, but this is what I know of the human body and the way it works, and I do have a diploma in anatomy and physiology.

As any woman will tell you when you have a baby it is the time when you push the hardest in your life, and I am not even sure a man can push as hard as a woman because there would never be any reason he would have to. I used to know a woman who had bad constipation all the time like Elvis and one day when she hadn't been for ages, she pushed that hard her bowel came out of her body with the solid faeces, but never did her intestines push up against her heart and stop it from beating, why because it is impossible.

In the diagram of the human male, you will notice that between the heart and the intestines there are, the stomach, the liver, the kidneys, the spleen, the pancreas, bile duct, duodenum, and the gall bladder, all kept nicely away from the heart and lungs by our diaphragm, and then our heart, which is not made clear in this diagram, is tucked away almost behind our left lung and has a sack of its own protecting it, so nothing that might be floating around in the body, if that were possible, could ever get to the heart, and when you push down, you fill your lung pushing your diaphragm down giving even more protection to your heart, so unless Elvis was hanging upside down by his toes, which I think I can in all honesty say he wasn't, there is no way his intestines could have pushed up and stopped his heart, if he was pushing that hard he would of had a prolapse of the bowel like the person I told you about. So next time you hear someone say this you can tell them that it would be physically impossible, even for Elvis, he was murdered plain and simple.

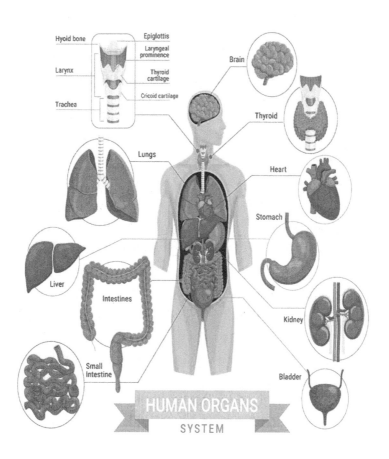

Hyoid bone • Epiglottis • Laryngeal prominence • Larynx • Thyroid cartilage • Cricoid cartilage • Trachea • Brain • Thyroid • Lungs • Heart • Stomach • Liver • Intestines • Kidney • Small Intestine • Bladder

HUMAN ORGANS
SYSTEM

NICK ADAMS

If we can all agree that Parker and the mob were behind the murder of Elvis, where they also behind the murder of Nick Adams. Nick is said to have died of an over-dose, his family said he would never do that, and we know they tried to make it look like Elvis had overdosed too, now I know some of you will think I am jumping at shadows, and I have no real evidence just a gut feeling and timing.

Parker had worked long and hard to manipulate Elvis's image from that of the "rebel" of the 50s to the "all American boy" and "apple pie" rolled into one, Parker got Elvis drafted, no matter that Elvis did not want to be drafted and it led to his mother dying sooner, what Parker wanted Parker got, he also got rid of Larry from Elvis's circle of friends by literally terrorising him and his family by having his house ransacked while Parker pretended to be nice buying his children ice-creams according to Larry in one of his books. Just like Parker never allowed Elvis to have any contact with Steve Binder after the 68 special even though Elvis desperately wanted to, Elvis had disobeyed Parker and paid the price.

Parker had finally got Elvis married and not only did the apple pie now have custard but a cherry on the top, Lisa. Parker's goal was complete, it did not matter that Elvis had fought off marrying

Cilla for years, in the end Parker always got what he wanted. I also think Parker successfully covered up Cilla knocking Elvis out cold in the bathroom by not allowing anyone except his spy Joe and Cilla and Parkers doctors to see him, had he really cared about Elvis he would have been in hospital having his skull x-rayed. Elvis always said he was hit on the head from behind, he did not trip over a flex as we were told.

Most think Nick and Elvis's friendship died off in the fifties, but that is not true Elvis often talked to Nick by phone and when he was in LA he would go visit him, but he had to keep it quiet because Parker did not approve, just like he did not approve of Larry. Now as I said timing is everything, Lisa was born on the 1st of March 1968, less than a month before Nick Adams supposedly took his own life on the 7th of February 1968. The big question is why would Nick do that, the official answer is he was depressed that his career was not going well, but the truth is he had a tell-all manuscript/book about all the hell-raising he and Elvis had got up to in the late 50s. Now I do not know how Parker found out, I don't know if Nick approached Parker about it thinking he could get money from Parker to delete the more risqué parts, or if Parker found out some other way, but either way Nick had the foresight to hide the manuscript which wasn't found till years later by his daughter who published it, but it was heavily redacted/edited by all accounts. So why would

Nick kill himself when he had this book to get published, which even back then would have made him a fortune, I seriously do not think Nick killed himself at all, I think Parker with the mobs blessings had Nick murdered, could you imagine if that book had come out just after Lisa was born, all Parkers work to make Elvis wholesome would have been gone, undone in one foul swoop, so Nick had to go. The fact is Nick had hid his book so well it wasn't found and published till 2012, the official line is Nick wrote it in the late 1950s, but if that was true why didn't he get it published back then, why when he had around ten years to publish it did he not do so, especially if his acting career was ending, as we have been led to believe was the reason for his over-dose, none of it makes any sense at all, except the timing, that he should die just before Lisa was born. I also think over time Elvis realised Parker had had Nick killed which was why he did everything he could to keep Parker happy, he knew what a vicious man he could be, am I mad, maybe, or maybe not.

Elvis with Nick while he was filming "Follow that Dream" in 1961, as you can see they were still friends

THIS IS MY MURDER THEORY

I think this is what happened to Elvis, this is my opinion, my theory, I must make that clear as several times when I first said I though Elvis had been murdered, I was threatened over it, but we are all allowed to have our own opinions on things, and this theory is mine.

Firstly, Elvis had no intention of dying, he had made lots of plans for his and Lisa's future which really started when he changed his will in March 77, not only did he remove Cilla from his will, but he removed all the hangers-on and leeches, he had finally allowed himself to see the truth of who and what they were. There are scurrilous rumours that Vernon removed pages because none of the leeches could believe Elvis did not leave them anything, but the truth is Elvis did not leave them anything, all the pages are numbered so no one could have removed pages without changing the page numbers and they were not changed. Others have said there were two wills, but legally it is always the last will which is the one that is legal. What Elvis did do was have prevision for his grandmother and Aunt Delta included and for no one else. Elvis left everything to Lisa specifically, but on page 4 the will says "of each of my children" this is extremely important, had he thought he was about to die he would have just left it all to Lisa but Elvis thought he was going to live for many more years get married and have more children, so when anyone says he changed his will

[317]

because he knew he was going to die you can tell them that is not right and why. He also had Charlie witness the will because he knew Charlie was the only person he could trust not to tell anyone else, and he had Ginger witness it to proving that by March he had no intention of marrying her as someone who is a witness cannot profit from the will.

Most people do not have any idea of this, but I have been told by several sources that Elvis was owned by the mob/mafia, there are several books about the mob killing Elvis, but Elvis was effectively owned by the mob as soon as he signed with Parker, I think. In Elaine Dundy's book "ELVIS and GLADYS" she writes about an article with mob undertones warning Elvis to keep his mouth shut and not to do or say anything he should not, whilst in the army, she says the article in Billboard magazine said that "High on Presley's agenda, is extensive dental and periodontal (gum) work" but there was nothing wrong with Elvis's teeth, this apparently is mafia/mob code for keeping your mouth shut. So, Elvis would have been aware he was owned, and his career or life was not his own, he was trapped.

In Larry Geller's book "IF I CAN DREAM" pages 183/4 he tells a story of Elvis meeting some businessmen, and how afterwards Elvis was nervous and said to Larry, "Larry it's a dangerous universe, it's dangerous no matter who you are, the higher you are the more dangerous it is, in the twenties and thirties the gangs would mow you down in the streets or they'd dump your body in the river. Now these people are legitimate businessmen. They're businessmen who run the corporations. They own great things in America, so they go about things a different way now. They're very nice, they negotiate, and they'll let you talk."..... talking of Sam Cocke's murder Larry says, now and again Elvis would allude to it and after he was refused "permission" to tour outside the country the subject rose again. "Why do you think Sam Cocke is dead?" he asked me "Everyone thinks he was murdered in a motel. Oh, he was murdered all right. He was murdered because he got out of line. I got it straight from the horse's mouth. Cocke was told that he had a big mouth, to stay in line, and he didn't do it. You can go so far Larry; you can go so far." Larry also tells of a story in his book about when he is with Elvis and Elvis suddenly could not breathe and Elvis said to Larry "they've given me the wrong meds, I'm gonna die", now in Larrys story of course Elvis did not die, but it is very similar to what happened when Elvis did die. After reading this I am more convinced than ever that the mob did indeed have Elvis murdered, they controlled RCA, they controlled Parker and they controlled Elvis, I have been told. When Elvis said he was going to quit touring and Vegas and take time out in Hawaii to get fit and then go into movies they had no time left for Elvis, he was worth more dead than alive to them, have you never thought it amazingly convenient that they had all those records and souvenirs ready to sell the moment Elvis died, because they knew when it was going to happen, they orchestrated it I think. I have been told RCA was about to go bankrupt, and I have been told apart from the massive sales they got because of Elvis's death they also had a million-dollar insurance policy on Elvis, so his death stopped RCA from going bankrupt, if Elvis had just retired from touring and making records and done serious acting as he wanted, RCA would have gone under.

I originally thought it was a hitman who had done the deed but now I do not for several reasons, 1) because I do not think a hit man could have walked into Elvis's bathroom without all hell breaking loose, but someone he knew could have, someone who thought Elvis would already be asleep as he knew Elvis had already taken his sleep meds. 2) an old article I have recently read were one of the MMs is trying to pin the blame on Elvis's dentist, when we know Elvis's dentist had said he never prescribed Elvis codeine because he knew Elvis was allergic to it, then in another interview Joe said Elvis murdered himself over Cilla and he, Joe, destroyed the suicide note, which we know is ludicrous, amazing how he still kept on changing his story. 3) when an attacker/murderer destroys someone face it is nearly always personal, 4) this person knew Elvis was allergic to codeine and more importantly that it gave him breathing difficulties, 5) there was a person who was suing

Elvis and I have been told was desperate for money, and 6) the tree branch.

Like most people for a long time I believed the official version of Elvis's death but certain things kept on nagging at me, and over the last few years I have spoken to several people who knew Elvis, and I read a lot of things about it and this is what I think happened and why it happened, and I know a lot will disagree and will not like what I have to say, but I have the right to my theory, my opinion, and a lot of other people including Vernon thought Elvis was murdered by someone he knew. Was it murder or dereliction of duty at the very least, someone who was supposed to be in charge who got paid for making sure Elvis was safe should have been charged with manslaughter in my opinion.

You may find this upsetting. When you read this remember that Elvis was supposed to be checked on every thirty minutes when he had a girlfriend with him or more often if he was alone. Elvis had sleepwalked since a child and was once found on a fire escape sleepwalking, but on this day, no-one checked on him, why?

There are many reasons I think Parker had Elvis killed. Elvis had planned to end his relationship with Parker when his contract expired with Parker, Joe was always Parkers mole and Elvis had fired Joe once before in the 60s for telling Parker his personal things. I think Joe told Parker when he heard Elvis discussing his plans for his future with Larry Geller while on holiday in

Hawaii in March 1977. This is evidenced by the fact Parker tried to sell Elvis' contract in April but could not get anywhere near enough money for it to pay off his considerable gambling debts. I have been told Parker was always a mob man and we all know a dead star is worth so much more than one in semi-retirement.

I had often wondered why Elvis had not sacked Parker many years before but have learned from the book "Elvis and Gladys" that Parker was blackmailing Elvis. Early on in Elvis's career Parker found out that Elvis's father and uncle had been to jail and used this knowledge to make Elvis do whatever he wanted. Elvis was convinced no one would like him if they found out he had a father and uncle who were jailbirds, remembering how judgemental people were of Elvis in the early days, burning effigies of him and his records, even banning him in some places, calling him a bad influence on the young, even devils spawn, you can understand Elvis's concerns. So Elvis was terrified of Parker telling the world, not even his closest friends new about it, but after the Wests and Hebler wrote their book and Elvis saw the manuscript, Elvis knew if his fans would stick with him after that then they would if they knew his father had been to jail and it gave him the courage to finally leave Parker and look for a new manager which is what I think got Elvis killed. Elvis had plans to stop touring, he had already stopped Vegas, and to go to Hawaii and get fit. Elvis had a new manager lined up Tom Hulett and he wanted to go back into movies, Elvis always wanted to be recognised as a great actor, maybe even direct. His ultimate goal was to get full custody of Lisa, something he knew he could not do while he was touring, as Lisa was only happy when she was with him. The tour dates after he died were to be his last and that is why he had to be killed then because that would be the last time his killers would be at Graceland because they were going to be fired at the end of the tour.

The things that don't add up that day are many, but for me the one that stands out the most is the fact no one checked on Elvis. He was supposed to be checked every half an hour if he was with a girl or every ten minutes if he wasn't. He had suffered from sleepwalking since a child, he even had a bed in his dressing room for someone, but between 7-30am and 2-30pm, this time now seems to be fluid, no one in the house checked on him. Ricky was supposed to be on duty, but everyone knew he was high and out of it somewhere and Al Strada had been brought in to do Ricky's job that day, but Joe kept him busy doing other things, I have been told Elvis' Aunt Delta had to take him his sleeping medication because of this, so they all knew Ricky was not looking after Elvis. Elvis must have been dead for at least two hours when emergency services were called. I have also been told Elvis called down at 7-30am and his Aunt Delta went across to the Jiffy Mart and got Elvis some buttermilk and a newspaper he had asked for. She took it up to Elvis in his room and gave it to him along with his sleeping meds, but she did not see or hear Ginger. I have my doubts as to whether Ginger was even there, and there are a few reasons, firstly Elvis phoned his friend Nurse Cocke in the hospital around 9am to ask her to go see him, saying he was alone and needed a woman to talk to, and she said she would go round after her shift. Why would he say that if Ginger was in bed he would just go wake her up, also one of the maids heard Ginger in her bathroom having a shower, it was separate to Elvis' in the early afternoon, it would seem she had a shower, got dressed put her make-up on and made two phone calls as she says in her book, one to her mother and one to her friend before she went looking for Elvis. You would think the first thing she would do would be find out if Elvis was ok if you woke to find his side of the bed had not been slept in. I have also been told she also had had an affair with David Stanley, and he had been seen that day taking someone into Graceland covertly. Elvis even had Ginger followed when she went to nightclubs because he was sure she was having an affair with someone.

Another one of the great mysteries is the amount of codeine that the toxicology report said Elvis had in his system. It was apparently 10 times a normal therapeutic dose, which is twenty tablets, he would have found it impossible to keep down long enough for it to have been digested and absorbed into his system, they would have made him throw them all up. Several people have said he was allergic to it, the first time he was given it was in the army, that's when he discovered he was allergic to codeine, it not only made him sick and give him a rash it also made it hard for him to breathe, so no way would he take it knowingly. He also would not take it because it makes you constipated and he suffered from acute constipation all his life, so no way he would take something in that high dose that would make it much worse. Even for those who are not allergic to it, it is notorious for making people vomit, so no way could Elvis have kept that amount down. I believe his attacker injected Elvis with it during the attack. When the EMTs got there they said the bathroom was a mess, things had been knocked over and in disarray as if a fight had taken place. Elvis liked everywhere to be neat and tidy, yet by the time the police detectives got there not only was everything tidy even Elvis' vomit had been cleaned up. Why had there only been a police officer placed on the main stairs, why not in the bathroom itself and on the back staircase as well to preserve the scene.

It has been estimated that Parker owed anywhere up to 50 million to the mob in gambling debts, you can read it was nothing for him to lose a million in one night at Vegas. I have been told Elvis even had one of his FBI friends investigating Parker, Elvis also had FBI undercover agents in his band in Vegas so they could spy on the mob. Unfortunately for Elvis the mob knew it, and so when Parker told them Elvis would no longer be playing Vegas, bringing in the crowds, he was of no further use to them. Plus, Elvis and his father were due to testify in an FBI sting about a jet called "Operation Fountain Pen".

Joe either lied or changed his statements a lot about that day. Firstly, he said he had found Elvis in bed, then it was Ginger who found Elvis in the bathroom, and I have now been told it was Al who found Elvis in the bathroom. Joe in one statement also said he had tried to give Elvis mouth to mouth which is bogus because the EMTs said lividity was fixed and rigor had set in. In fact, one said he was that dark blue he thought it was a black man to start with, hence we know Elvis must have been dead at least two hours. So no way could Joe have opened his mouth to give him mouth to mouth, then there is the story that Joe smashed in Elvis's teeth in order to give him mouth-to-mouth (as written in the book A Southern Life), in the MMs book Billy Smith says he asked Patsy who was there, and Joe did smash in Elvis's face, but why would he do that to someone who was obviously dead, and even if he were not dead but had lockjaw you would breathe into his nose to get air into his lungs not smash his teeth and risk choking him, the only reason I can think someone would do that is to hide the damage done to Elvis's face during the fight.

Also note there was NO evidence Elvis had been on the toilet if you get my drift. Elvis often used his bathroom as a reading room, he had an old barber's chair in there he would use to sit on when he read, and Elvis had told Ginger he was going in there to read, so why was this story invented and that image and put it in everyone's head, I have been told by several people about Elvis's reading chair and also in the MMs book Lamar Fike says because of the position of the body Elvis had to of been in his reading chair. I have been told the lie was spread so people would know the king had been dethroned, that it was a mob signature, and another final insult to Elvis.

So, the scene was set, Joe kept everyone busy downstairs, and sent Al, who was supposed to be there to be Elvis's valet, on an errand leaving the murderers enough time to go upstairs and murder Elvis. Elvis was feeling groggy, half asleep from the sleep meds he had taken earlier. The coroner's report said Elvis had suffered a broken nose and cheekbone, which they said was due to him falling off the toilet, but he had NOT been on the toilet. Don't forget Elvis' bathroom had a thick shag pile carpet in it so no way did he do that much damage to his face falling off the toilet even if he had been on it and as I said there was no evidence he had been on the toilet. He also had carpet fibres in his mouth and nose as if someone had held his face down into the carpet. I think he sustained the injuries in the attack, (moreover when someone tries to destroy someone else's face in an attack it is nearly always because they are jealous of that person and do not want anyone to see them as attractive ever again, which we know several of the MMs were). I have also been told that the heavy gold chain Elvis was wearing had cut into the flesh of Elvis's neck like someone had used it as a garrotte.

I think this is what happened, Elvis was seated on his old barber's chair where he had been reading, feeling groggy, half asleep, with his eyes closed, when the attackers entered the bathroom and quietly walked over, possibly one of them saying 'it's only me boss' so Elvis would not bother opening his eyes. They tried to inject Elvis with a syringe of codeine, Elvis went into fight or flight mode, Elvis threw his book and a struggle ensued which is why so many things got knocked off the counter, (they were probably expecting Elvis to be fully asleep from the meds). Elvis then tried to use the phone near to his chair only to find it out of order, so he then pushed the buzzer that went direct to Charlie's room, but Charlie was not there, (I have been told he was at the gate talking to fans.) Elvis lunged toward the bathroom door as the first injection started to take effect, Elvis fell to his knees crawling, (which is why his PJ bottoms came down) as he threw up, one of the attackers then grabbed the back of Elvis's head in one hand and pulled back on the chain with the other twisting it to tighten it around Elvis's neck and then slammed his face into the floor which broke his nose and cheekbone, and then wrenched Elvis's head back ferociously with such force that he snapped Elvis's neck. Dr Nick in the video says Elvis's neck was broken. When someone breaks someone else's face on purpose it is nearly always personal, and just to make sure he could not breath one of them held his face down in the carpet which is how Elvis got the carpet fibres in his mouth and nose, gasping for his last breath. A hit-man would not have needed to be so brutal he would have been able to subdue Elvis while he injected him, but these attackers could not do that and smashed Elvis's face, then injected Elvis with the rest of the codeine/nitrate as he lay dying, now the investigator said he could not find any needle marks, but the syringes found at the scene where the type used for soft tissue like a dentist uses in the mouth, now there are lots of soft tissue areas on a body, there was blood in Elvis's nose so they could have injected him there, or his mouth, or ear, don't forget his pants were down so they could have injected him in those soft tissue areas which would never be seen.

In Donna Presley's book she says that Vernon said Elvis died of anaphylactic shock, because he was allergic to codeine it would not have had to have been a large dose to kill him, but as there were two empty syringes left there, so it is not a leap to think they injected him twice to make sure he would die. I think they left the empty syringes without needles and cartridges to make it look like Elvis had overdosed but he would not of have had time to have disposed of the needles and cartridges while he was dying. The toxicology report confirms there was codeine in Elvis's blood though it does not say how much like the earlier report did. I now think there were possibly three assailants, one an older MM who stood watch and his brother and the other a younger member of Elvis's crew who did the deed, of course I cannot say the names, but I think most will guess. The other big question is Elvis carried a gun everywhere with him, he had had so many death threats, he even took one to bed, so why didn't he have one in the bathroom with him, I have been told Ginger said there was an unloaded one there, but that does not make sense, an unloaded gun is useless, unless the perpetrators knew where Elvis had it and got to it before he did, then emptied it, and left it there.

Only after Elvis had been taken to hospital and pronounced dead and Joe had phoned Parker to tell him did Joe change his statement about how Elvis had been found. Then he told the world Elvis had been found with his pants down, something no one had to know, but I have learned it is a sign of a mob hit. Apparently, they did something similar to Sonny Liston. It is the final insult on the person, and saying he had been on the toilet they were basically saying the king had been dethroned. Sadly, once a slur on someone's character like that is made it sticks no matter what the evidence to the contrary is. Also, the coroner's report was not done properly. They did not take any photos which is and was standard procedure. They 'lost' his stomach contents and pronounced the cause of death before toxicology was done and yet they removed his brain looking for the reason Elvis's heart stopped but could not find anything. Why would they do that to someone who they seem to have said had had a heart attack, but in actuality the words they used just meant Elvis's heart had stopped, well everyone's heart stops when they die, so that means they did not actually give a cause of death, in fact they are known to have said they could find any reason why Elvis died. Which is why Vernon had a separate autopsy done. We know from several sources that Elvis had almost bit through his tongue and his eyes were protruding and I have been told the heavy gold chain he was wearing had been pulled so tight it had cut into the skin on his neck, these are obvious signs he was strangled, but that possibility was never mentioned, why didn't the coroner check to see if Elvis's hyoid bone had been broken which nearly always happens when someone is strangled.

It has been stated when they told Vernon his first words were "They have killed my boy". Vernon had his autopsy report done which is sealed till 2027 and had his own people investigate Elvis' death, Al Strada was the only one of the MMs Vernon trusted enough to help him after Elvis died. Vernon then had the bodies of Elvis and his mother moved to Graceland so they could not be got at. I think Vernon knew it was the mob behind it, Vernon knew who had done the actual deed and wanted to 'take care of them' his way but never had the chance before he died and to protect the family, he had the autopsy sealed. Remember how Parker dressed for the funeral in a Hawaiian shirt and shorts like he was going on holiday, in Alanna Nash's book she says how Parker acted strangely and could not look at the casket and would not be a pallbearer, she also says Vernon thought it was either Parker or one of Elvis's entourage who killed Elvis. At the funeral a tree branch broke and fell it just missed Joe apparently, I am sure it was Elvis trying to send a message to us all.

Elvis did ask Cilla if she would remarry him, not because he wanted her but because it was an easy way to get Lisa full time, he told Cilla it would be an open marriage with no strings, because he really did not want her near him and he knew she would be off doing her thing most of the time, he thought Cilla would jump at the chance but she did not, now you have to remember Cilla still thought she was going to inherit everything, Cilla had no clue that Elvis had changed his will and removed her from it, it's why he had Ginger and Charlie witness it cause he knew neither they would tell Cilla. Now although Elvis had no intention by this point of marrying Ginger, he knew Ginger would never be a stay at home wife and mother as she could never wait to get away from Elvis, and made him feel like crap, but because he was annoyed Cilla turned him down he told her he was going to marry Ginger before the end of the August tour, as I said to annoy Cilla, not thinking that Cilla might in some way take revenge on him for it. That is why Elvis was murdered when he was, it had to be done then to make sure Cilla got the inheritance she thought she was getting, and before he had the chance to fire most of the hangers-on, he was about to fire Parker, Joe, Fike, the Stanleys and many others if he gave up touring and could not afford to have them hanging around. Don't forget how close Cilla was to Joe and Parker, even Tom Hanks said he was amazed at how well Cilla spoke of Parker, for Parker it would have been best to wait till the end of the tour, but if Elvis had married Ginger like he threatened to, to annoy Cilla, every dynamic would have changed. I am sure Cilla must have told Joe what Elvis had said to her, don't forget Joe tried to peddle the theory that Elvis overdosed because Cilla would not remarry him, and Joe said he had found the letter and burnt it. Remember Cilla told Kardashian she would not remarry till after Elvis was dead, that is because she was positive Elvis was going to leave everything to her, it would have meant she could have resigned Elvis's contract that was about to end with Parker and Cilla did keep Parker on, and she wouldn't have fired Joe like Elvis was about to, also remember that when she was on the plane going to the funeral Cilla thought it was all hers, according to Suzanne Finstad's book 'Child Bride' and was ordering everyone around, and she was reported as saying it was the best day in her life. So now she is tied into it, little did she know that not only had Elvis written her out of his will but that he had no intention of marrying Ginger whatever happened.

The attacker had a brother who often helped out at Graceland and did so that day, there was not one attacker, I think there were three. Something else that has been bothering me, Joe said he was busy downstairs packing Elvis's things for the tour, what exactly was he packing Elvis only wore four jumpsuits for of 1977, it could not have been Elvis's clothes because they were upstairs in Elvis's dressing room right next to his bathroom, which would have meant Joe would have seen Elvis in the bathroom. As I said this is my theory/opinion, like the pieces of a jigsaw this is how I think they go together and with each new piece I find the picture becomes clearer, I could be wrong, it could have been someone else, but one thing for sure is, things that day do not add up. Elvis had had two physicals a couple of weeks before he died, one was for Lloyds of London and this one had him running on a treadmill whilst hooked up to an ECG machine and his heart was fine, now if anything had been wrong with his heart it would have shown up on that ECG I would have thought, so why did his heart suddenly and for no apparent reason the coroner could find, stop. Also a lot has been made in the media about the contents of Elvis's intestines, there are many exaggerated claims about the size and the length of time Elvis had gone without a bowel movement, but the fact is this, when Elvis had his physicals they also included an x-ray of his intestines, which if you have ever had one you know you have to take barium meal beforehand, and your intestines have to be empty, so that means two weeks before he died Elvis's intestines were empty, and anyone who looks can tell they were at his last concert on the 26th June 1977 as well and as I have already said Dr. Francisco said in a Memphis newspaper that "Elvis did not have an impacted colon at the time of his death."

In Ginger's book she says Vernon asked her about syringes, but she does not elaborate, do you know who else died of a sudden unexpected heart attack and on the anniversary of Elvis's death, Ginger's husband, not long after she had published her book, I was told it a sign to her from the mob not to talk, or did he commit suicide as one of Gingers cousins have said, but to actually die of natural causes on the same day as Elvis, the odds are astronomical.

Do not forget Elvis also had a substantial amount of codeine in his blood which he would not have ever taken and even if he did it would of had to of been injected cause his stomach would not of had time to metabolise that many pills, and there were two metal cartridge syringes found at the scene, Dr Nick in his book said Dan Warlick the investigator went over Elvis's body with a fine tooth-comb looking for injection sites but could not find any, but there are places where they would not be seen, like under Elvis's tongue, in his nostrils, both his nose and mouth had been severely damaged so finding a needle puncture mark would have been very hard. You also need to know Elvis did not keep any medication in his room at all, it was brought to him when he needed it, his nurse, Tish, kept all Elvis's meds, and they gave them to Elvis in an envelope when he needed them so no way could he have mistakenly downed a bottle of anything by accident like some people have said.

In Stephen Ubaney's book "Who murdered Elvis" the investigator Dan Warlick says this on the corners report on Elvis, note Elvis did not die of a heart attack, in fact, his cause of death was inconclusive, another words they could not find out why Elvis was dead, but because of media pressure and a possible conspiracy they made it appear he had died of a heart attack but he did not "As investigator Dan Warlick returned to the hospital with his information from the death scene and shared his findings with Jerry Francisco, he found the Medial Examiner uninterested and all but cut him off in mid-sentence. Then he asked Warlick if he would like to attend the autopsy. No less than nine doctors with a combination of 147 years of practical experience lined both sides of the porcelain autopsy table in anticipation of answering the ultimate question: What happened to this man? Each doctor had his own specialty and was hand-picked to perform his specific duty in the investigation into each of Elvis Presley's vital organs. Among them were Dr. Eric Muirhead, Chief of Pathology at Baptist Memorial Hospital, and a full Professor of Pathology at the University of Tennessee Medical School. Muirhead, in fact, was recognized as Francisco's senior. Dan Warlick slipped into a white laboratory coat and joined the autopsy team as they readied their gleaming instruments around Elvis's body, but he was met with a tremendous feeling of shock. After all, this was not just any man – this was Elvis Presley. Elvis, who was the idol of millions of fans around the world, was actually lying on this table. The whole incident was very hard to digest as the former Rock-n-Roll rebel of the 1950s lay naked, bulbous and coloured blue/black from the death process. As the high-pitched clanging of metal instruments being laid into position occurred so did the harsh reality that less than 12 hours earlier, these men would have been asking for autographs, now they were preparing to cut Elvis' body apart. Two worlds had collided in the most bizarre and unusual way and here Elvis was staring the doctors blankly and lifelessly in the eyes. As the shock of the famous corpse slowly departed, Warlick got down to the usual business of inspecting the corpse before the procedure could begin. Thompson and Cole's The Death of Elvis tells it like this: "Warlick checked Elvis' nose, observed a trickle of blood seeping from the nostrils...He did note that the body had 'congestion to the face and upper torso.' Warlick looked into Elvis' mouth. He saw the teeth had been smashed in the attempts to put a tube down Elvis' throat, but he saw no evidence of choking or vomiting. Putting these indicators together, the doctors estimated that Elvis might have died as early as 9:00 a.m. "

After Warlick completed his inspection, Elvis was lifted onto a very thick cork board used for the dissection of internal organs. Nearly two hours into the procedure, all of Elvis' organs had been removed, including his brain, which they had meticulously sectioned and analysed. However, none of the doctors in the team could come up with a reason why Elvis shouldn't be back on stage. Another pathologist named Noel Florendo was brought onto the team for his expertise with the electron microscope. Florendo's job was to remain at his workstation and analyse specimens from various tissues. But when it came time for Elvis' heart to be sectioned and analysed, Dr. Florendo and Warlick couldn't resist inspecting the organ themselves. As the clock continued to tick and the sun fell on the extensive and ongoing medical investigation, it became obvious that no answers would be established until a later date. Earlier in the day, Francisco had committed to a scheduled press conference at 8:00 p.m. and as the time drew near, the world held its collective breath, but still the autopsy team had no idea what killed Elvis. Nonetheless, the TV press conference began. Before any samples could be tested or results tallied, Jerry Francisco pronounced to the waiting world that Elvis Presley had died of 'cardiac arrhythmia due to undetermined heartbeat.' In other words, Elvis died because his heart stopped beating. Upon this comment Francisco's superior at the hospital, Dr. Muirhead, nearly fell over backwards in his chair. He simply couldn't believe what just came out of Francisco's mouth. Rather than tell the world that the autopsy was "inconclusive pending further tests", Francisco told a bigger story than Mother Goose."

Also remember when Elvis died all the police in Memphis were put on high alert, they feared the fans would riot if anything but a death from natural causes had been said was the cause of death, it should have been left as an open verdict as there was NO cause of death found, I think there was a lot of pressure to issue the death as natural because of the fear the fans would go crazy.

I hope this once and for all stops the naysayers, it is official Elvis did not abuse drugs sadly this did not make the headlines of all the major newspapers or gutter press it's not as sensational as saying he was a drug addict but this is proof he was not an addict and he did not abuse drugs, shame on all of you who think so, final diagnosis proves drugs did not kill the king. In 1978 Utah paper Salt Lake City newspaper sited. "When he died, Elvis Presley's body contained 11 drugs - including morphine,

Valium, codeine, and barbiturates but a new and decisive study done at the Presley family request proves beyond doubt that drugs were not responsible for his death". Elvis was not a junkie, as some scandal magazines have tried to say. "We have not detected any drug in Elvis that doesn't have a medical rationale to it - only agents prescribed for perfectly normal, rational medical reasons," explains Dr. Bryan S. Finkie, director of the University of Utah's Centre for Human Toxicology. The Utah Centre was called into the Presley case to do a third toxicological survey of materials taken from Elvis during the family requested autopsy. This study is the most accurate and decisive of the three performed. Other, more hurried investigations showed there were between eight and 10 drugs present in Presley's system at the time of death, and the earlier investigations left open the possibility the drugs may have caused the famed singer's death. The other toxicological studies were done by Baptist Memorial Hospital, Memphis, Tenn., and Bio-Science Laboratories, Van Nuys, Calif. They requested the Utah Centre (which has an internationally famous reputation) complete the study and make the final determination. Although the Utah Centre receives some federal funds, it does not have to make public its findings. This is an exclusive report based on an interview with Dr. Finkle. Presley family privacy rights prevail, and there are no legal duties to make the information public. Dr. Finkle answered some questions, and the two-page report based on his findings - which he wrote at Bio-Science's request - satisfied Shelby (Tenn.) County Medical Examiner Dr. Jerry T. Francisco that Elvis' death was not from a drug overdose or even from having a large number of drugs present in his body at one time. Presley's Death Certificate was signed before Dr. Finkle's full report was finished, but Francisco consulted Dr. Finkle by phone before signing. The completed, written report satisfied Francisco he was correct in stating on the Death Certificate that drugs did not contribute to Elvis' death. The Utah Centre's study backed up earlier findings that four drugs were present in significant quantities - the sedatives Ethinamate and Methaqualone, the narcotic codeine and barbiturates, or "downers". Four other drugs were found in smaller amounts - the antihistamine chlorpheniramine, the tranquilizers Valium and the painkillers meperidine and morphine. Morphine, however, was not taken by Presley - it was a codeine by-product. Three other drugs were found in trace amounts, but one thing the Utah Centre was asked to look for - Ritalin, a trade name for the notorious stimulant methylphenidate - was not found. Immediately after his death, Presley's family requested an autopsy be performed on Elvis. It was decided two labs would survey the autopsy materials. Dr. Finkle's final word on the subject is, "As a toxicologist, if you ask me why he had the drugs in his system the answer is that he needed them medically. All the drugs were in a range consistent with therapeutic requirements for known conditions of illnesses which he had." Presley illnesses included hypertension, cardiovascular compromisee and a colon obstructino. Official cause of death was listed as hypertensive heart failure with coronary artery disease a contributing factor. The University of Utah lab report, based on months of exhaustive, comprehensive testing, confirms that original diagnosis.

(NEWS SOURCE: Utah Paper Salt Lake City Newspaper) This toxicology report also is in Dr,Nicks book.

In Donna Presley's book 'Precious Memories' she says this, Vernon said he thought someone Elvis knew had swapped Elvis's meds with codeine knowing he was allergic to them, and that Elvis went into anaphylactic shock and had a slow and painful death, Vernon not knowing who he could trust wanted to 'take care' of the culprits himself, so he knew who it was, though he never told Donna, sadly he died before he could TCB as he said Elvis would want him to do. We know Elvis had twenty times the normal amount of codeine in his bloodstream, and that Elvis was allergic to codeine. We also know he showed many signs of strangulation, but these signs also are often the same in anaphylactic shock, which it says about in the autopsy that Vernon had sealed according to Donna Presley's book.

To Summarise

When someone is strangled or goes into anaphylactic shock, several things happen as they die, their eyes bulge, they bite down that hard on their tongue they can bite through it, and in men their genitals enlarge. Elvis almost bit through his tongue but not quite, his eyes were bulging and apparently his gentles enlarged, and Elvis had blood in his nostril as well. The detective Dan Warlick said he found two cartridge-type syringes in the bathroom, and this is important, neither of them had any cartridge in them or a needle either. He said he checked over Elvis's body for any puncture marks and did not find any. That type of syringe is used to go into soft tissue, like a dentist uses, now Dan Warlick could not have possibly checked inside Elvis's mouth because rigor mortice had set in and as I said Elvis had bitten down on his tongue, so even if someone had injected Elvis in the mouth it would have been obscured. The detective did not say if he had shone a light up Elvis's nose, only that there was blood and carpet fibres there, so once again, the injections could have taken place there. Neither did he say if he had checked any other soft tissue areas like deep into the ear, or in Elvis's gentles which would explain the trousers being down as well. There is no possible way that Elvis could have injected himself as he would have gone into shock almost immediately and not been able to remove the empty cartridges and needles and dispose of them somewhere other than the bathroom, so someone else must have done it. Warlick did say he thought the syringes might have been left there to make people think Elvis had accidentally over-dosed, but that would have been impossible, because no way could Elvis have tidied up after himself. When Elvis was first given codeine in the army, he found it immediately hard to breathe, so with twenty times the therapeutic dose in his system he would have been fighting for breath and his life straight away, so if nothing else convinces you Elvis was murdered this should. You know my theory and we know who was there that day, we know Charle could never have done it and Vernon must have trusted Al Strada because he kept him on to help him investigate, so that really only leaves the house staff and I am pretty sure it was not them, and a few MMs and a brother of one of them, who I was told personally was there. It is a shame not more people have taken what Donna has said more seriously and nothing was ever done while it could have been done, but the world still needs to know the truth and as I have also said in the past Vernon kept the autopsy secret to protect Lisa and others has also been verified in Donna Presley's book for me. Dr Nick also made a video saying he thought Elvis's neck may have been broken, there are also other videos on this playlist including Joe lying about how he found Elvis. Anaphylactic is almost impossible to detect after death, which is another reason they got away with it.

You may or may not know this but often suspects in a murder investigation will offer up other people as culprits for who did it, trying to deflect the investigation away from them. This has happened twice since Elvis died both Joe E. and David S. have accused Elvis of killing himself, I will leave you to draw your own conclusions.

I have been told Vernon laid a single red rose every day on Elvis's grave, and often spent the rest of the day in Elvis's bedroom crying for his son.

ELVIS AARON PRESLEY

https://pubmed.ncbi.nlm.nih.gov/10823122/

https://www.youtube.com/playlist?list=PLjE_RQ2
rCyrklmhG2r9lZhPtX7ix17eVV

https://elvisdecoded.com/2023/03/01/q3-
impacted/?fbclid=IwAR3RDDpm4OyokujdIEbe2
NYx_NgWeFRVOpIJUSME2F9AqCLhTGigLtd_
ZJg